624.0289 CON
REF

ITEM NO: 1924780
WA 1405571 6

Health and Safety Testing in Construction for the Professionally Qualified Person

2007 Edition Issue 2

constructionskills

D1494186

Published by ConstructionSkills
Bircham Newton, King's Lynn
Norfolk PE31 6RH

First Published 2006

Revised 2007

14055716

University of
South Wales
Prifysgol
De Cymru

Library Services

© Construction Industry Training Board 2007

The Construction Industry Training Board otherwise known as CITB-ConstructionSkills and ConstructionSkills is a registered charity (Charity Number: 264289)

ISBN: 978-1-85751-215-1

ConstructionSkills has made every effort to ensure that the information contained in this publication is accurate. It should be used as guidance material and not as a replacement for current regulations or existing standards.

All rights reserved. No part of this publication may be reproduced, stored in a retrieval system, or transmitted in any form or by any means, electronic, mechanical, photocopying, recording or otherwise, without the prior permission in writing of ConstructionSkills.

Produced by Thomson Prometric
Printed in the UK

Contents

UNIVERSITY OF WALES, NEWPORT
LIBRARY AND INFORMATION SERVICES
ALLT-YR-YN

Introduction

The ConstructionSkills Health and Safety Test has seen significant growth since its introduction six years ago.

Major industry bodies and construction employers are driving health and safety as a top priority, and embracing the test as a key tool in achieving this awareness.

During the last few years there have been a number of important developments, including the introduction of mobile testing vehicles to widen testing capacity in response to the industry's need for site-based skills assessment. More recently, we introduced the SkillsDirect service, which ties health and safety more closely to the process of getting qualified and carded – taking us a step closer to the industry vision of a fully qualified workforce. This will also assist companies and individuals in demonstrating their competence, as required by the 2007 revision of the CDM regulations.

The result is that we now test more than 300,000 candidates per year and we recently celebrated the one millionth Test pass. An achievement the industry can be proud of.

The introduction of the ConstructionSkills Health and Safety Test for the Professionally Qualified Person is a significant marker in the Test's history, extending the scope of the Test to the non-site based professionals who contribute so much to the industry and who have a significant impact on health and safety on site.

We are extremely pleased to have had the support we have had from this sector, with key industry bodies getting involved in setting the standards for the test, ensuring it meets the needs of the sector. We thank them for this input, and look forward to their continued support.

On that point, I'm very pleased that Keith Clarke, CEO of Atkins, has agreed to write the foreword for this question book to add his view on the significance of the test to this sector of industry.

Sir Michael Latham
Chairman
ConstructionSkills

Foreword

The expectation that the construction industry is inherently dangerous is finally changing due to the efforts of all parts of the industry. It is vital we provide a safe and dignified working environment that all involved can feel proud of.

The role of off-site professionals in raising the health and safety agenda – whether they are architects, engineers, quantity surveyors or the many other disciplines involved in the design and procurement process – is significant and, until recently, underestimated. The introduction of the ConstructionSkills Health and Safety Test for the Professionally Qualified Person will now address this gap, and should have enormous influence, not just on the construction techniques used, but also on the values and ethos of the sites themselves.

Safety is not about policing but about behaviour and the broad and deep consensus that unsafe sites or activities are simply unacceptable in any circumstances. This is the responsibility of us all.

Getting a CSCS or affiliated card is a strong sign that a fully trained workforce is key and that we all, as professionals, need to show leadership by example and not be escorted visitors on our own sites.

We have a great industry – it must become a healthy and safe one for all those working in it.

Keith Clarke
Chief Executive
Atkins Group

Preparing for the Health and Safety Test

For many years the construction industry has had more than its fair share of serious accidents and deaths. Lack of training and little awareness of danger have been factors that have contributed to this unacceptable accident record with many accidents occurring because the same mistakes are repeated over and over again.
The ConstructionSkills Health and Safety Test helps raise standards across the industry by ensuring that workers meet a minimum level of health and safety awareness before going on site. It now forms a key part of most major card schemes, including CSCS and its affiliates.

The test has been running for over five years and underwent significant improvements including an enhanced delivery infrastructure in April 2005*. The addition of the Professionally Qualified Person Test ensures the test continues to meet the needs of our industry.

* Health and Safety Test questions and answers do change from time to time in line with regulations. ConstructionSkills will make every effort to keep the test book up-to-date. ConstructionSkills will not test any candidates on any questions that are no longer in line with legislation and will not test any candidates on any questions that do not feature in the most up-to-date published book.

This guide has been written to help you prepare for the Professionally Qualified Person Health and Safety Test.
You will see that the guide is divided into two main areas:

- **Professional core questions**
  Sections 1 – 18

- **Specialist test questions**
  Sections 19 – 20

Each test will comprise 50 questions: 40 from the Professional core, with at least 1 from each section, plus 10 from either of the Specialist sections.
You will be allowed 45 minutes for the test.

Preparing for the Health and Safety Test

The Professionally Qualified Person test consists of 40 questions from the Professional core (Sections 1–18) and 10 from a Specialist section. Anyone engaged in a design activity, as broadly defined by the CDM Regulations, should sit the 'Professionally Qualified Person – Design' specialist section. All other professionally qualified persons who need to visit sites as part of their roles should sit the more general 'Professionally Qualified Person' specialist section.

You should read through this guide and attempt some of the questions from each section before attending the test. This will give you an idea of your strengths and weaknesses, and indicate the areas where you may need to improve your knowledge.
You can also attend one of the courses run by our National Construction College – call us on 08457 336666 to find out more.

The purpose of the test is to help reinforce the existing health and safety knowledge of professionally qualified persons who, although engaged in the project, are not based on site. Legislation and professional Codes of Conduct place obligations upon professionally qualified people to assess a situation and respond in an appropriate way. The Health and Safety Test for the Professionally Qualified Person helps provide information on common site hazards and how the professional person may be expected to react.

The self-employed

Many of the questions will refer to the duties of employers. In law, the self-employed have the same legal responsibilities as employers. To keep the questions as brief as possible, the wording only refers to the duties of employers, and not to the duties of the self-employed, but the questions apply to both.

Your level of knowledge

In sitting the Professionally Qualified Person Test it will be expected that you have a working knowledge of the CDM Regulations. It is also expected that you will have prepared yourself for the Health and Safety Test by using the revision material contained in this book.

Northern Ireland legislation

All questions in this book are based on British legislation. However, Northern Ireland legislation may differ from that in the rest of the UK.

For practical reasons, all candidates (including those in Northern Ireland) will be tested on questions using legislation relevant to the rest of the UK only.

Booking your Health and Safety Test

The easiest ways to book your test are online or by telephone. You will be given the date and time of your test immediately. The test can also be booked by postal/fax application. You should expect that tests will be available 3 to 8 weeks from when you book.

The test is offered in over 150 Thomson Prometric test centres throughout the UK. The list of centres is available online at **www.citb-constructionskills.co.uk/hstest**

What you need to be able to make a booking

To make a test booking you will need

1. Your ConstructionSkills registration number – new applicants will be able to register by calling **0870 600 4020**.
   If you have previously booked a test with us or are a member of CSCS, you will be asked to provide your individual ID number.
2. To know which category of test you need to take i.e. 'Professionally Qualified Person' or 'Professionally Qualified Person – Design'.
3. A method of payment – credit or debit card for online, telephone, post or fax bookings, or a cheque or postal order if sending your application.

Online

You can make, check or change a test booking 24 hours a day, 7 days a week at **www.citb-constructionskills.co.uk/hstest**

You will receive an email confirming your test booking along with directions to the test centre. It is important that you check the details in this confirmation and follow any instructions it gives regarding the test.

Telephone

To book your test by telephone, call:

0870 600 4020

The registration centre is open between 8am and 6pm, Monday to Friday. All the details of your test will be confirmed with you during the call and again in a letter that you should receive within 10 days. It is important that you check the details in this confirmation and follow any instructions it gives regarding the test.

By post/fax

If you prefer to book by post or fax you need to use the application form available at **www.citb-constructionskills.co.uk/hstest** or by calling **0870 600 4020**. If you are making a booking for a group of candidates please ask for the Group Booking application form.

Special needs

If you have any special requirements for taking the test, such as reading difficulties or preferring to take the test in a language other than English, please advise us at the time of booking.

Corporate Mobile Testing and Internet Based Testing Centres

For organisations wishing to test a group of candidates at their place of work, please call 0161 868 9255 for details of the corporate mobile testing service or becoming an internet based test centre.

What if I don't receive a confirmation letter?

If you do not receive a confirmation letter within the time specified, please telephone 0870 600 4020 to check that your test booking has been made.

We cannot take responsibility for postal delays. If you miss your test event, you will unfortunately forfeit your fee.

How do I cancel or postpone my test?

To cancel or postpone your test you should go online or call the booking number at least three clear working days before your test date, otherwise you'll lose your fee.

Only in exceptional circumstances, such as documented ill health or family bereavement, can this rule be waived.

Taking your Health & Safety Test

Please allow plenty of time to get to the test centre as you may not be able to take the test if you arrive after your session has started. You should also ensure that you bring all relevant documentation with you or you will not be able to sit your test and you will lose your fee.

You will need:

- your confirmation email or letter
- ID bearing your photo and signature (e.g. driving licence or passport)
- any other items listed on your confirmation letter.

When you arrive at the test centre please follow the ConstructionSkills or Thomson Prometric branded signs. Upon arrival, the test centre staff will check your documents and ensure you are booked onto the correct category of test.

Remember

- **no photo**
- **no signature**

NO TEST

During the test

The tests are all delivered on a computer screen. However you do not need to be familiar with computers, and the test does not involve any writing. All you will need to do is select the relevant answer boxes, using either a mouse or by touching the screen.

Before the test begins you can sit a practice session to get used to the way the test will work.

The test will contain a number of multiple-choice questions. Most questions will give four answers, only one of which is correct. You must select the answer that you think is correct. Some questions will require you to select two correct answers from four or five, and others require three correct from a choice of five. Each question will be clearly marked with the number of correct answers that you must find.

You will be allowed 45 minutes for the test.

At the end of the test there is an optional survey which gives you the chance to provide feedback on the test process.

If you fail the test you will receive feedback on the section in which you got questions wrong before leaving the test centre. If you do not reach the required standard you are strongly advised to read again all of the topic areas appropriate to your test. If you fail the test, you'll have to wait at least three clear working days before you take the test again.

Obtaining your CSCS Professionally Qualified Person Card

It is becoming increasingly important to carry the right card to prove your skills on construction sites.

Once you have passed your Health and Safety Test, you should apply to join the appropriate card scheme for your trade. In most cases, this will be CSCS (Construction Skills Certification Scheme) or an affiliated scheme.

Your pass letter should include contact details of all relevant schemes you can apply to.

You can find out more about many of the schemes at **www.citb-constructionskills.co.uk/cardschemes**

Scheme contact details

To contact CSCS, which covers most schemes in the industry, telephone **0870 417 8777** or go to **www.cscs.uk.com**

All candidates will be asked questions from the Core test sections, which include:

- Section 1 General Responsibilities
- Section 2 Accident Prevention and Reporting
- Section 3 Health and Welfare
- Section 4 Manual Handling
- Section 5 Working at Height
- Section 6 Personal Protective Equipment (PPE)
- Section 7 Emergency Procedures and First Aid
- Section 8 Safe Use of Hazardous Substances
- Section 9 Electrical Safety and Hand Tools
- Section 10 Fire Prevention and Control
- Section 11 Safety Signs and Signals
- Section 12 Site Transport, Plant and Lifting Operations
- Section 13 Noise and Vibration
- Section 14 Excavations and Confined Spaces
- Section 15 Supervisory and Management
- Section 16 Demolition
- Section 17 Plumbing or Gas
- Section 18 Highway Works

General Responsibilities

1.1

During site induction, you do not understand something the presenter says. What should you do?

- [ ] A: Attend another site induction
- [ ] B: Ask the presenter to explain the point again
- [ ] C: Guess what the presenter was trying to tell you
- [ ] D: Wait until the end then ask someone else to explain

1.2

What is a **toolbox talk**?

- [ ] A: A short training session on a particular safety topic
- [ ] B: A talk that tells you where to buy tools
- [ ] C: Your first training session when you arrive on site
- [ ] D: A sales talk given by a tool supplier

1.3

A Permit to Work allows:

- [ ] A: the emergency services to come on to the site after an accident
- [ ] B: certain jobs to be carried out under controlled conditions
- [ ] C: HSE inspectors to visit the site
- [ ] D: untrained people to work without supervision

1.4

Now that work on site is moving forward, the safety rules given in your site induction seem out of date. What should you do?

- [ ] A: Do nothing, you are not responsible for safety on site
- [ ] B: Speak to the site manager about your concerns
- [ ] C: Speak to your colleagues to see if they have any new rules
- [ ] D: Decide yourself what to do to suit the changing conditions

1.5

You are aware that a Prohibition Notice has been placed on some site equipment. What does this mean?

- [ ] A: It must not be used unless the operatives are supervised
- [ ] B: It must not be used until serious safety issues have been rectified
- [ ] C: It can only be used under the supervision of an HSE inspector
- [ ] D: Only supervisors can use it

Answers: 1.1 = B, 1.2 = A, 1.3 = B, 1.4 = B, 1.5 = B

1.6

If you discover children playing on site, what is the first priority?

- A: Tell the site manager
- B: Phone the police
- C: Ensuring the safety of the children
- D: Find out how they got on to the site

1.7

When should you report environmental incidents and near misses that occur on site?

- A: Never
- B: During your next break
- C: As soon as practical
- D: At the end of the day

1.8

Where should rubbish or other leftover materials be put at the end of a job? It should be:

- A: left where it is
- B: picked up and thrown with rubbish left by other people
- C: put in a designated waste area
- D: picked up and dumped outside the site

1.9

Before you are allowed to start work for the first time on a new site you should:

- A: sign in at security
- B: be shown where the toilets and drinking water are
- C: be given safety wellingtons
- D: receive induction training

1.10

Checking your identity and the purpose of your visit before allowing you on site:

- A: is part of the contractor's controls to ensure that the public does not get on site
- B: is a waste of time and petty bureaucracy
- C: enables the client to check up on you to see if you earned your fee
- D: is an example of security measures being too strict

Answers: 1.6 = C, 1.7 = C, 1.8 = C, 1.9 = D, 1.10 = A

2

Accident Prevention and Reporting

2.1

Which of these does not have to be recorded in the accident book?

- [ ] A: Your national insurance number
- [ ] B: The date and time of your accident
- [ ] C: Details of your injury
- [ ] D: Your home address

2.2

A scaffold has collapsed and you saw it happen. When you are asked about the accident, you should say:

- [ ] A: nothing, you are not a scaffold expert
- [ ] B: as little as possible because you don't want to get people into trouble
- [ ] C: exactly what you saw
- [ ] D: who you think is to blame and how they should be punished

2.3

What is the most important reason for keeping your work area clean and tidy?

- [ ] A: To prevent slips, trips and falls
- [ ] B: So that you don't have a big clean-up at the end of the week
- [ ] C: So that waste skips can be emptied more often
- [ ] D: To recycle waste and help the environment

2.4

If you have a minor accident, who should report it?

- [ ] A: Anyone who saw the accident
- [ ] B: A sub-contractor
- [ ] C: You
- [ ] D: The HSE

2.5

How would you expect to find out about health and safety rules when you first arrive on site?

- [ ] A: During site induction
- [ ] B: In a letter sent to your home
- [ ] C: By reading your employer's health & safety policy
- [ ] D: By asking others on the site

Answers: 2.1 = A, 2.2 = C, 2.3 = A, 2.4 = C, 2.5 = A

2.6

A near miss is an incident where:

- [ ] A: you were just too late to see what happened
- [ ] B: someone could have been injured
- [ ] C: someone was injured and nearly had to go to hospital
- [ ] D: someone was injured and nearly had to take time off work

2.7

If you cut your finger and it won't stop bleeding, you should:

- [ ] A: wrap something around it and carry on working
- [ ] B: tell the site manager
- [ ] C: wash it clean then carry on working
- [ ] D: find a first-aider or get other medical help

2.8

The work of a contractor is affecting your safety. What should you do?

- [ ] A: Go home
- [ ] B: Speak to the site manager
- [ ] C: Speak to the contractor's supervisor
- [ ] D: Speak to the contractor who is doing the job

2.9

If your doctor says that you have Weil's disease, you will need to tell your employer. Why?

- [ ] A: Your employer will not want to go anywhere near you
- [ ] B: Your employer will have to report it to the HSE
- [ ] C: Your colleagues might catch it from you
- [ ] D: The whole site will have to be closed down

2.10

Why is it important to attend site induction?

- [ ] A: You will get to know other new starters
- [ ] B: Risk assessments will be handed out
- [ ] C: Site specific health and safety rules will be explained
- [ ] D: Permits to work will be handed out

Answers: 2.6 = B, 2.7 = D, 2.8 = B, 2.9 = B, 2.10 = C

3

Health and Welfare

3.1

Direct sunlight on bare skin can cause:

- [ ] A: dermatitis
- [ ] B: rickets
- [ ] C: acne
- [ ] D: skin cancer

3.2

You need to handle a hazardous substance. You should wear the correct gloves to help stop:

- [ ] A: skin disease
- [ ] B: vibration white finger
- [ ] C: Raynaud's Syndrome
- [ ] D: arthritis

3.3

Your doctor has given you some medication. Which of these questions is the most important?

- [ ] A: Will it make me sleepy or unsafe to work?
- [ ] B: Will I work more slowly?
- [ ] C: Will my supervisor find out?
- [ ] D: Will I oversleep and be late for work?

3.4

Someone goes to the pub at lunchtime and has a couple of pints of beer. What should they do next?

- [ ] A: Drink plenty of strong coffee then go back to work
- [ ] B: Stay away from the site for the rest of the day
- [ ] C: Stay away for an hour and then go back to work
- [ ] D: Eat something, wait 30 minutes and then go back to work

3.5

Exposure to engine oil and other mineral oils can cause:

- [ ] A: skin problems
- [ ] B: heart disease
- [ ] C: breathing problems
- [ ] D: vibration white finger

Answers: 3.1 = D, 3.2 = A, 3.3 = A, 3.4 = B, 3.5 = A

3.6

You can get occupational dermatitis from:

- [ ] A: hand-arm vibration
- [ ] B: another person with dermatitis
- [ ] C: some types of strong chemical
- [ ] D: sunlight

3.7

You can catch an infection called tetanus from contaminated land or water. How does it get into your body?

- [ ] A: Through your nose when you breathe
- [ ] B: Through an open cut in your skin
- [ ] C: Through your mouth when you eat or drink
- [ ] D: It doesn't, it only infects animals and not people

3.8

Exposure to which of the following may not result in lung disease?

- [ ] A: Asbestos
- [ ] B: Bird droppings
- [ ] C: Steam
- [ ] D: Silica dust

3.9

Pigeon droppings and nests are found in an area where you are required to work. You should:

- [ ] A: carry on with your work carefully
- [ ] B: stop work and seek advice
- [ ] C: try to catch the pigeons
- [ ] D: let them fly away before carrying on with your work

3.10

Very dirty hands should be cleaned with:

- [ ] A: soap and water
- [ ] B: thinners
- [ ] C: white spirit
- [ ] D: paraffin

Answers: 3.6 = C, 3.7= B, 3.8 = C, 3.9 = B, 3.10 = A

3.11

To help keep rats away from sites, everyone on site should:

- [ ] A: buy rat traps and put them around the site
- [ ] B: ask the local authority to put down rat poison
- [ ] C: bring a large cat to site
- [ ] D: do not leave scraps of food lying around

3.12

When should operatives use barrier cream?

- [ ] A: Before they start work
- [ ] B: When they finish work
- [ ] C: As part of first aid treatment
- [ ] D: Always if gloves have not been provided

3.13

You find that toilets on site are dirty. What should you do?

- [ ] A: Ignore the problem, it is normal
- [ ] B: Make sure that you tell the site manager who can sort it out
- [ ] C: Find some cleaning materials and do it yourself
- [ ] D: See if you can use the toilets in a nearby café or pub

3.14

You are more likely to catch Weil's disease (Leptospirosis) if you:

- [ ] A: work near wet ground, waterways or sewers
- [ ] B: work near air conditioning units
- [ ] C: work on building refurbishment
- [ ] D: drink water from a standpipe

3.15

Breathing in a dusty atmosphere for long periods can cause:

- [ ] A: occupational asthma
- [ ] B: occupational dermatitis
- [ ] C: skin cancer
- [ ] D: glue ear

Answers: 3.11 = D, 3.12 = A, 3.13 = B, 3.14 = A, 3.15 = A

3.16

White spirit or other solvents should not be used to clean hands because:

- [ ] A: they strip the protective oils from the skin
- [ ] B: they remove the top layer of skin
- [ ] C: they block the pores of the skin
- [ ] D: they carry harmful bacteria that attack the skin

3.17

Which of the following is a legal requirement for the site welfare facilities?

- [ ] A: Wholesome drinking water
- [ ] B: Somewhere to take a rest
- [ ] C: Suitable and sufficient lighting
- [ ] D: All of the other answers

Answers: 3.16 = A, 3.17 = D

Manual Handling

4.1

To lift a load, you should always try to:

- [ ] A: stand with your feet together when lifting
- [ ] B: bend your back when lifting
- [ ] C: carry the load away from your body at arm's length
- [ ] D: divide large loads into smaller loads

4.2

You need to lift a load from the floor. You should stand with your:

- [ ] A: feet together, legs straight
- [ ] B: feet together, knees bent
- [ ] C: feet slightly apart, knees bent
- [ ] D: feet wide apart, legs straight

4.3

To lift a load safely, you need to think about:

- [ ] A: its size and condition
- [ ] B: its weight
- [ ] C: whether it has handholds
- [ ] D: all of the other answers

4.4

When you lift a load manually, you must:

- [ ] A: keep your back straight and use the strength in your leg muscles to lift
- [ ] B: make sure there are always two people to lift the load
- [ ] C: use a crane or another lifting device to pick up the load
- [ ] D: move the load as quickly as possible

4.5

Your new job involves some manual handling. An old injury means that you have a weak back. What should you do?

- [ ] A: Tell your supervisor you can lift anything
- [ ] B: Tell your supervisor that lifting might be a problem
- [ ] C: Try some lifting then tell your supervisor about your back
- [ ] D: Tell your supervisor about your back if it gets injured again

Answers: 4.1 = D, 4.2 = C, 4.3 = D, 4.4 = A, 4.5 = B

4.6

If you have to twist or turn your body when you lift and place a load, it means:

- [ ] A: the weight you can lift safely is **less** than usual
- [ ] B: the weight you can lift safely is **more** than usual
- [ ] C: nothing, you can lift the **same** weight as usual
- [ ] D: you **must** wear a back brace

4.7

You have to move a load that might be too heavy for you. You cannot divide it into smaller parts and there is no one to help you. What should you do?

- [ ] A: Do not move the load until you have found a safe method
- [ ] B: Get a forklift truck, even though you can't drive one
- [ ] C: Try to lift it using the correct lifting methods
- [ ] D: Lift and move the load quickly to avoid injury

4.8

Who should decide what weight can be lifted safely?

- [ ] A: The person performing the lift
- [ ] B: Their supervisor
- [ ] C: Their employer
- [ ] D: The HSE

Answers: 4.6 = A, 4.7 = A, 4.8 = A

LIB

Working at Height

5.1

How many people should be on a ladder at the same time?

- [ ] A: 2
- [ ] B: 1
- [ ] C: 1 on each section of an extension ladder
- [ ] D: 3 if it is long enough

5.2

A scaffold guard-rail must be removed to allow you to carry out a survey. You are not a scaffolder. Can you remove the guard-rail?

- [ ] A: Yes, if you put it back as soon as you have finished
- [ ] B: Yes, if you put it back before you leave site
- [ ] C: No, only a scaffolder can remove the guard-rail but you can put it back
- [ ] D: No, only a scaffolder can remove the guard-rail and put it back

5.3

Who should check a ladder before it is used?

- [ ] A: The person who is going to use it
- [ ] B: A site supervisor
- [ ] C: The site safety officer
- [ ] D: The manufacturer

5.4

What is the best way to make sure that a ladder is secure and won't slip?

- [ ] A: Ensure it is tied at the top
- [ ] B: Ask someone to stand with their foot on the bottom rung
- [ ] C: Tie it at the bottom
- [ ] D: Wedge the bottom of the ladder with blocks of wood

5.5

You need access to work at height. It is not possible to install fall prevention. What should you do?

- [ ] A: Hold onto something while you use your other hand to make notes
- [ ] B: Ask someone to hold you while you make notes
- [ ] C: Providing you have been trained, wear a harness and lanyard and fix it to an anchor point
- [ ] D: Tie a rope round your waist and tie the other end to an anchor point

Answers: 5.1 = B, 5.2 = D, 5.3 = A, 5.4 = A, 5.5 = C

5.6

Which of the following is NOT an appropriate indicator that a scaffold is safe to use?

- [ ] A: An up-to-date inspection log
- [ ] B: A joint inspection with a competent person
- [ ] C: An up-to-date scafftag
- [ ] D: Other people are using it

5.7

Before you climb any ladder on site you should make sure that it is:

- [ ] A: aluminium
- [ ] B: hired
- [ ] C: secured
- [ ] D: painted

5.8

To ensure the safety of people who have to gain access to a place of work at height, ladders are:

- [ ] A: always acceptable for work below 2 metres
- [ ] B: all right to use if it gets the job done more quickly
- [ ] C: generally the least favoured option
- [ ] D: now banned on all sites

5.9

Work at height is:

- [ ] A: only work carried out above 2 metres
- [ ] B: only work carried out on a scaffold
- [ ] C: banned under the Work at Height Regulations
- [ ] D: to be avoided where possible

5.10

If you see an unguarded opening in a floor whilst you are on site, your first priority is to:

- [ ] A: stop any work going on around it and immediately report it to the site manager
- [ ] B: ensure the opening is where it should be on the drawings
- [ ] C: measure the opening and check it against the bill of quantities
- [ ] D: do nothing: work on site is the sole responsibility of the contractor

Answers: 5.6 = D, 5.7 = C, 5.8 = C, 5.9 = D, 5.10 = A

5.11

Whilst visiting a site, what action should you take if something falls from a scaffolding nearly hitting you?

- [ ] A: Gain access to the scaffold and investigate the problem
- [ ] B: Not walk near that part of the scaffolding again
- [ ] C: Ensure you are wearing your hard hat
- [ ] D: Immediately clear other people from the area and report the near-miss to the site manager

5.12

Your organisation's policy is to avoid walking on fragile roof materials. A common example of fragile roof material is:

- [ ] A: asphalt felt roof
- [ ] B: asbestos cement sheets and rooflights
- [ ] C: raised seam roof
- [ ] D: single-ply membrane

5.13

Which of the following provides effective protection against falls when roofwork is underway?

- [ ] A: Only using experienced operatives
- [ ] B: Workers staying away from the edge of the roof
- [ ] C: Edge of the roof clearly marked with flicker tape
- [ ] D: Suitable edge protection in place

5.14

If a working platform is 4 metres above the ground, the foot of the access ladder should be placed:

- [ ] A: 1 metre out
- [ ] B: 2 metres out
- [ ] C: 3 metres out
- [ ] D: 4 metres out

5.15

What should be included in a safety method statement for working at height? Give three answers.

- [ ] A: The cost of the job and time it will take
- [ ] B: The sequence of operations and the equipment to be used
- [ ] C: How much insurance cover will be required
- [ ] D: How falls are to be prevented
- [ ] E: Who will supervise the job on site

5.16

Scaffold towers may be erected by:

- [ ] A: anyone who has the instruction book
- [ ] B: anyone who is competent and authorised
- [ ] C: advanced scaffolders only
- [ ] D: an employee of the hire company only

Answers: 5.11 = D, 5.12 = B, 5.13 = D, 5.14 = A, 5.15 = B,D,E, 5.16 = B

5.17

A competent person must routinely inspect a scaffold:

- [ ] A: after it is erected and at intervals not exceeding 7 days
- [ ] B: only after it has been erected
- [ ] C: after it is erected and then at monthly intervals
- [ ] D: after it is erected and then at intervals not exceeding 10 days

5.18

When covering rooflights, what two requirements should the covers meet?

- [ ] A: They are made from the same material as the roof covering
- [ ] B: They are made from clear material to allow the light through
- [ ] C: They are strong enough to take the weight of any load placed on it
- [ ] D: They are waterproof and windproof
- [ ] E: They are fixed in position to stop them being dislodged

5.19

What is the main reason for using a safety net or inflatable air bags rather than harness and lanyard?

- [ ] A: Safety nets or air bags are cheaper to use
- [ ] B: A safety harness can be uncomfortable to wear
- [ ] C: Harnesses and lanyards have to be inspected
- [ ] D: Safety nets or air bags are collective fall arrest measures

5.20

What is the main reason for not allowing debris to gather in safety nets?

- [ ] A: It will overload the net
- [ ] B: It looks untidy from below
- [ ] C: It could injure someone who falls into the net
- [ ] D: Small pieces of debris may fall through the net

Answers: 5.17 = A, 5.18 = C,E, 5.19 = D, 5.20 = C

5.21

You are working at height, but the securing cord for a safety net is in your way. What should you do?

- [ ] A: Untie the cord, carry out your work and tie it up again
- [ ] B: Untie the cord, but ask the net riggers to re-tie it when you have finished
- [ ] C: Tell the net riggers that you are going to untie the cord
- [ ] D: Leave the cord alone and report the problem

5.22

Ideally, a safety net should be rigged:

- [ ] A: immediately below where you are working
- [ ] B: 2 metres below where you are working
- [ ] C: 6 metres below where you are working
- [ ] D: at any height below the working position

5.23

What is the main danger of leaving someone who has fallen suspended in a harness for too long?

- [ ] A: They will become bored
- [ ] B: They may try to climb back up the structure and fall again
- [ ] C: They may suffer severe discomfort and lose consciousness
- [ ] D: It is a distraction for other workers

5.24

What is the recommended maximum height for a freestanding mobile tower when used indoors?

- [ ] A: There is no height restriction
- [ ] B: Three lifts
- [ ] C: As specified by the manufacturer
- [ ] D: Three times the longest base dimensions

5.25

After gaining access to the platform of a mobile tower, the first thing you should do is:

- [ ] A: check that the tower's brakes are locked on
- [ ] B: check that the tower has been correctly assembled
- [ ] C: close the access hatch to stop people or equipment from falling
- [ ] D: check that the tower does not rock or wobble

Answers: 5.21 = D, 5.22 = A, 5.23 = C, 5.24 = C, 5.25 = C

5.26

Edge protection is designed to:

- [ ] A: make access to the roof easier
- [ ] B: secure tools and materials close to the edge
- [ ] C: stop rainwater running off onto workers below
- [ ] D: prevent people and materials falling

5.27

Before climbing a ladder you notice that it has a rung missing near the top. What should you do?

- [ ] A: Do not use the ladder and immediately report the defect
- [ ] B: Use the ladder but take care when stepping over the position of the missing rung
- [ ] C: Turn the ladder over so that the missing rung is near the bottom and use it
- [ ] D: Attempt an improvised repair by lashing something across the stiles

5.28

When can someone who is not a scaffolder remove parts of a scaffold?

- [ ] A: If the scaffold is not more than 2 lifts in height
- [ ] B: As long as a scaffolder refits the parts after the work has finished
- [ ] C: Never, only competent scaffolders can remove the parts
- [ ] D: Only if it is a tube and fittings scaffold

5.29

How far should a ladder extend above the stepping-off point if there is no alternative, firm hand-hold?

- [ ] A: 3 rungs
- [ ] B: 2 rungs
- [ ] C: 1 metre
- [ ] D: Half a metre

5.30

When using ladders for access, what is the maximum vertical distance between landings?

- [ ] A: 5 metres
- [ ] B: There is no maximum
- [ ] C: 9 metres
- [ ] D: 30 metres

Answers: 5.26 = D, 5.27 = A, 5.28 = C, 5.29 = C, 5.30 = C

5.31

On a working platform, the maximum permitted gap between the guard-rails is:

- [ ] A: 350mm
- [ ] B: 470mm
- [ ] C: 490mm
- [ ] D: 510mm

5.32

When should guard-rails be fitted to a working platform?

- [ ] A: If it is possible to fall 2 metres
- [ ] B: At any height if a fall could result in an injury
- [ ] C: If it is possible to fall 3 metres
- [ ] D: Only if materials are being stored on the working platform

5.33

Before starting work at height, the weather forecast says the wind will increase to 'Force 7'. What does this mean?

- [ ] A: A moderate breeze that can raise light objects, such as dust and leaves
- [ ] B: A near gale that will make it difficult to move about and handle materials
- [ ] C: A gentle breeze that you can feel on your face
- [ ] D: Hurricane winds that will uproot trees and cause structural damage

5.34

A 'Class 3' ladder is:

- [ ] A: for domestic use only and must not be used on site
- [ ] B: of industrial quality and can be used safely
- [ ] C: a ladder that has been made to a European Standard
- [ ] D: made of insulating material and can be used near to overhead cables

5.35

How will you know the maximum weight or number of people that can be lifted safely on a mobile elevating work platform?

- [ ] A: The weight limit is reached when the platform is full
- [ ] B: It will say on the Health and Safety Law poster
- [ ] C: You will be told during site induction
- [ ] D: From an information plate fixed to the machines

Answers: 5.31 = B, 5.32 = B, 5.33 = B, 5.34 = A, 5.35 = D

5.36

When is it most appropriate to use a safety harness and lanyard for working at height?

- [ ] A: Only when the roof has a steep pitch
- [ ] B: Only when crossing a flat roof with clear roof-lights
- [ ] C: Only when all other options for fall prevention have been ruled out
- [ ] D: Only when materials are stored at height

5.37

When is it safe to use a scissor lift on soft ground?

- [ ] A: When the ground is dry
- [ ] B: When the machine can stand on scaffold planks laid over the soft ground
- [ ] C: When stabilisers or outriggers can be deployed onto solid ground
- [ ] D: Never

5.38

You need to cross a roof. How do you establish if it is fragile?

- [ ] A: Tread gently and listen for cracking
- [ ] B: Look at the risk assessment or method statement
- [ ] C: Look at the roof surface and make your own assessment
- [ ] D: There is no need to do so if you walk along a line of bolts

5.39

After gaining access to a roof, you notice some overhead cables within reach. What should you do?

- [ ] A: Keep away from them while you work but remember they are there
- [ ] B: Confirm that it is safe for you to be on the roof
- [ ] C: Make sure that you are using a wooden ladder
- [ ] D: Hang coloured bunting from them to remind you

Answers: 5.36 = C, 5.37 = C, 5.38 = B, 5.39 = B

5.40

You have to lean over an exposed edge while working at height. How should you wear your safety helmet?

- [ ] A: Tilted back on your head so that it doesn't fall off
- [ ] B: Take your helmet off while leaning over then put it on again afterwards
- [ ] C: Wear the helmet as usual but use the chin-strap
- [ ] D: Wear the helmet back to front whilst leaning over

5.41

When trying to clip your lanyard to an anchor point, you find the locking device does not work. What should you do?

- [ ] A: Carry on working and report it later
- [ ] B: Tie the lanyard in a knot round the anchor
- [ ] C: Stop work and report to your supervisor
- [ ] D: Just carry on working without it

5.42

What of the following is a significant disadvantage of using an aluminium scaffold tower?

- [ ] A: The aluminium will corrode in the wet weather
- [ ] B: It can never be built more than 2 lifts high
- [ ] C: Materials cannot be stored on the working platform
- [ ] D: The lack of weight means it can be displaced by high winds

5.43

If someone is working from a cherry-picker, they should attach their safety lanyard to:

- [ ] A: a strong part of the structure that they are working on
- [ ] B: a secure anchorage point inside the platform
- [ ] C: a secure point on the bottom of the machine
- [ ] D: a scaffold guard-rail

Answers: 5.40 = C, 5.41 = C, 5.42 = D, 5.43 = B

5.44

When work is being carried out above public areas, your first consideration should be:

- [ ] A: to minimise the number of people below at any one time
- [ ] B: to prevent complaints from the public
- [ ] C: to let the public know what you are doing
- [ ] D: to prevent anything falling on to people below

5.45

What should be the first consideration of a cherry-picker operator if the wind speed increases significantly?

- [ ] A: To tie all lightweight objects to the hand-rails of the basket
- [ ] B: To decide whether the machine will remain stable
- [ ] C: To tie the cherry-picker basket to the structure being worked upon
- [ ] D: To clip their lanyard to the structure being worked upon

5.46

What should be the first action of someone who is working above a safety net system and finds a damaged net? They should:

- [ ] A: work somewhere away from the damaged area of net
- [ ] B: stop work and report it
- [ ] C: tie the damaged edges together using the net test
- [ ] D: see if they can get a harness and lanyard

5.47

If a safety lanyard has damaged stitching, the user should:

- [ ] A: use the lanyard if the damaged stitching is less than 2 inches long
- [ ] B: get a replacement lanyard
- [ ] C: do not use the damaged lanyard and work without one
- [ ] D: use the lanyard if the damaged stitching is less than 6 inches long

Answers: 5.44 = D, 5.45 = B, 5.46 = B, 5.47 = B

5.48

Which of these must happen before any roof work starts?

- [ ] A: A risk assessment must be carried out
- [ ] B: Those working on the roof must be trained in the use of safety harnesses
- [ ] C: Permits to work must be issued to those allowed to work on the roof
- [ ] D: A weather forecast must be obtained

5.49

A cherry picker has been hired-in to carry out a particular job. When fully extended it does not quite reach the required height. What would you expect the operator to do?

- [ ] A: Use a step-ladder on the machine platform
- [ ] B: Extend the machine fully and stand on the guard-rails
- [ ] C: Abandon the machine and use a long extending ladder
- [ ] D: Not to carry out the job until a safe alternative means of access has been established

5.50

In what circumstances is it acceptable to lower a MEWP, that is being operated at height, from its elevated position using the ground-level controls?

- [ ] A: If the person on the ground is trained and you are not
- [ ] B: In an emergency only
- [ ] C: If the operator needs to jump off the MEWP to gain access to the high-level work area
- [ ] D: If the operator needs both hands free to carry out the job in hand

5.51

When work is being carried out at height, which of these is the safest way to transfer waste materials to ground level?

- [ ] A: Through a waste chute directly into a skip
- [ ] B: Ask someone below to keep the area clear of people then throw the waste down
- [ ] C: Erect barriers around the area where the waste will land
- [ ] D: Bag or bundle up the waste before throwing it down

Answers: 5.48 = A, 5.49 = D, 5.50 = B, 5.51 = A

5.52

An outdoor tower scaffold has stood overnight in high winds and heavy rain. What should be done before the scaffold is used?

- [ ] A: Test that the brakes still work
- [ ] B: Tie the scaffold to the adjacent structure
- [ ] C: Ensure that the scaffold is inspected by a competent person
- [ ] D: Ensure that the platform hatch still works correctly

5.53

Scaffold inspections should be undertaken by:

- [ ] A: you when you visit the site
- [ ] B: a competent person
- [ ] C: someone who has attended a 'Scaffold Appreciation' course
- [ ] D: only by a scaffold company employee

5.54

Which of the following provides the public with adequate protection from falling objects?

- [ ] A: Big warning signs
- [ ] B: A worker in a hi-vis vest standing on the footway to warn people
- [ ] C: A viewing panel in the site hoarding
- [ ] D: A fan or scaffold 'tunnel' over the footway

5.55

All work at height must be:

- [ ] A: risk assessed and property planned
- [ ] B: only undertaken by scaffold contractors
- [ ] C: carried out as quickly as possible
- [ ] D: suspended if the forecast wind speed is above force 2

Answers: 5.52 = C, 5.53 = B, 5.54 = D, 5.55 = A

Personal Protective Equipment (PPE)

6.1

When should you wear safety boots or safety shoes on site?

- [ ] A: Only when you work at ground level
- [ ] B: In the winter
- [ ] C: Only when it is cold and wet
- [ ] D: All the time

6.2

To get the maximum protection from your safety helmet, you should wear it:

- [ ] A: Back to front, to stop the peak banging into things
- [ ] B: Pushed back on your head, to see better
- [ ] C: Square on your head, to stop it falling off
- [ ] D: Pulled forward, to protect your eyes

6.3

If your PPE gets damaged, you should:

- [ ] A: throw it away and work without it
- [ ] B: stop what you are doing until it is replaced
- [ ] C: carry on wearing it but work more quickly
- [ ] D: try to repair it

6.4

If there is a risk of materials flying into your eyes, you should wear:

- [ ] A: tinted welding goggles
- [ ] B: laser safety glasses
- [ ] C: chemical-resistant goggles
- [ ] D: impact-resistant goggles

6.5

Do all types of glove protect your hands against chemicals?

- [ ] A: Yes, all gloves are made to the same standard
- [ ] B: Only if you put barrier cream on your hands as well
- [ ] C: No, different types of glove protect against different types of hazard
- [ ] D: Only if you cover the gloves with barrier cream

Answers: 6.1 = D, 6.2 = C, 6.3 = B, 6.4 = D, 6.5 = C

6.6

You have been given a dust mask to protect you against hazardous fumes. What should you do?

- [ ] A: Do not start work until you have the correct RPE
- [ ] B: Do the job but work quickly
- [ ] C: Start work but take a break now and again
- [ ] D: Wear a second dust mask on top of the first one

6.7

You are about to start a job. How will you know if you need any extra PPE?

- [ ] A: By looking at your employer's health and safety policy
- [ ] B: You will just be expected to know
- [ ] C: From the risk assessment or method statement
- [ ] D: A letter will be sent to your home

6.8

You have been given disposable ear-plugs to use, but they keep falling out. What should you do?

- [ ] A: Throw them away and work without them
- [ ] B: Stop work until you get more suitable ones and are shown how to fit them
- [ ] C: Put two ear-plugs in each ear so they stay in place
- [ ] D: Put rolled-up tissue paper in each ear

6.9

Who has the legal duty to ensure that employees are provided with any PPE they need?

- [ ] A: Their employer
- [ ] B: The employees who need it
- [ ] C: A health and safety equipment supplier
- [ ] D: The person whose design created the need for the use of PPE

Answers: 6.6 = A, 6.7 = C, 6.8 = B, 6.9 = A

6.10

You have to work outdoors in bad weather. Your employer should supply you with waterproof clothing because:

- [ ] A: it will have the company name and logo on it
- [ ] B: you are less likely to get muscle strains if you are warm and dry
- [ ] C: you are less likely to catch Weil's disease if you are warm and dry
- [ ] D: the site manager will be able to see you more clearly in the rain

6.11

When should eye protection be worn?

- [ ] A: On very bright, sunny days
- [ ] B: If there is a risk of eye injury
- [ ] C: When it has been included in the bill of quantities
- [ ] D: Only for work with chemicals

6.12

Look at these statements about PPE. Which one is not true? Employees must:

- [ ] A: pay for any damage or loss
- [ ] B: store it correctly when it is not being used
- [ ] C: report any damage or loss to their manager
- [ ] D: use it as instructed

6.13

What features should you be looking for when obtaining wellington boots for a site visit?

- [ ] A: They must be black with a good sole pattern
- [ ] B: They only need a steel toe-cap
- [ ] C: They must have a steel toe-cap and mid-sole
- [ ] D: They must be smooth-soled to prevent the transfer of contaminated materials

6.14

You must wear high visibility clothing:

- [ ] A: when the need is identified in the contractor's or your employer's site rules
- [ ] B: only if you are inspecting deep excavations or tunnels
- [ ] C: during normal daylight hours only
- [ ] D: only if you are working alongside moving plant

Answers: 6.10 = B, 6.11 = B, 6.12 = A, 6.13 = C, 6.14 = A

7.1

If you want to be a first aider, you should:

- [ ] A: watch a first aider treating people then try it yourself
- [ ] B: ask if you can do a first aider's course
- [ ] C: buy a book on first aid and start treating people
- [ ] D: speak to your doctor about it

7.2

If you think someone has a broken leg, you should:

- [ ] A: lie them on their side in the recovery position
- [ ] B: use your belt to strap their legs together
- [ ] C: send for the first aider or get other help
- [ ] D: lie them on their back

7.3

If someone gets some grit in their eye, the best thing you can do is:

- [ ] A: hold the eye open and wipe it clean with tissue paper
- [ ] B: ask them to rub the eye until it starts to water
- [ ] C: tell them to blink a couple of times
- [ ] D: hold the eye open and flush it with clean water

7.4

Someone gets a large splinter in their hand. It is deep under the skin and it hurts. What should you do?

- [ ] A: Use something sharp to dig it out
- [ ] B: Make sure they get first aid
- [ ] C: Tell them to ignore it and let the splinter come out on its own
- [ ] D: Try to squeeze out the splinter with your thumbs

7.5

Someone has fallen from height and has no feeling in their legs. You should tell them to:

- [ ] A: roll onto their back and keep their legs straight
- [ ] B: roll on to their side and bend their legs
- [ ] C: stay where they are until medical help arrives
- [ ] D: raise their legs to see if any feeling comes back

Answers: 7.1 = B, 7.2 = C, 7.3 = D, 7.4 = B, 7.5 = C

Emergency Procedures and First Aid

7.6

Someone has got a nail in their foot. You are not a first aider. You must not pull out the nail because:

- [ ] A: you will let air and bacteria get into the wound
- [ ] B: the nail is helping to reduce the bleeding
- [ ] C: it will prove that the casualty was not wearing safety boots
- [ ] D: the nail is helping to keep their boot on

7.7

This sign means:

- [ ] A: first aid
- [ ] B: safe to cross
- [ ] C: no waiting
- [ ] D: wait here for help

7.8

You will find out about emergency assembly points from:

- [ ] A: a risk assessment
- [ ] B: a method statement
- [ ] C: the site induction
- [ ] D: the Permit to work

7.9

If someone burns their hand, the best thing you can do is:

- [ ] A: put the hand into cold water
- [ ] B: tell them to carry on working to exercise the hand
- [ ] C: rub barrier cream or Vaseline into the burn
- [ ] D: wrap your handkerchief around the burn

7.10

You have to work alone on a remote part of the site. What should your employer provide you with?

- [ ] A: A small first aid kit
- [ ] B: The first aid box out of the office
- [ ] C: Nothing
- [ ] D: A book on first aid

Answers: 7.6 = B, 7.7 = A, 7.8 = C, 7.9 = A, 7.10 = A

7.11

The first aid box on site is always empty. What should you do?

- [ ] A: Bring your own first aid supplies into work
- [ ] B: Find out who is taking all the first aid supplies
- [ ] C: Find out who looks after the first aid box and let them know
- [ ] D: Ignore the problem, it is always the same

7.12

When would you expect eye-wash bottles to be provided?

- [ ] A: **Only** on demolition sites where asbestos has to be removed
- [ ] B: **Only** on sites where refurbishment is being carried out
- [ ] C: On all sites where people could get something in their eyes
- [ ] D: On all sites where showers are needed

7.13

If someone is in contact with a live cable, the best thing you can do is:

- [ ] A: phone the electricity company
- [ ] B: dial 999 and ask for an ambulance
- [ ] C: switch off the power and call for help
- [ ] D: pull them away from the cable

7.14

What is the first thing you should do if you find an injured person?

- [ ] A: Tell the site manager
- [ ] B: Check that you are not in any danger
- [ ] C: Move the injured person to a safe place
- [ ] D: Ask the injured person what happened

7.15

Someone working in a deep manhole has collapsed. What is the first thing you should do?

- [ ] A: Get someone lowered into the manhole on a rope
- [ ] B: Climb into the manhole and give mouth-to-mouth resuscitation
- [ ] C: Run and tell the site manager
- [ ] D: Raise the alarm by shouting to let others know what has happened

Answers: 7.11 = C, 7.12 = C, 7.13 = C, 7.14 = B, 7.15 = D

7.16

How do you find out what to do if you are injured on site?

- [ ] A: By asking someone on site
- [ ] B: By looking for the first aid sign
- [ ] C: By attending a first aid course
- [ ] D: You are told at your site induction

7.17

In what way are site-based staff and visitors informed of the location of first aid facilities on site?

- [ ] A: By walking across the site looking for the first aid sign
- [ ] B: By searching the site office
- [ ] C: They are told during site induction
- [ ] D: By reading the Health and Safety Law poster

7.18

In which way should site visitors be informed of the actions to take in the event of an on-site emergency?

- [ ] A: They should study the plans on the wall of the site office
- [ ] B: They are informed during site induction
- [ ] C: They should ask the site manager
- [ ] D: They should take a look around the site for the emergency assembly point

7.19

How can you see for yourself that attention has been given to simple emergency procedures on site?

- [ ] A: Fire extinguishers are removed from fire points for safe keeping
- [ ] B: The distance between the structure and the assembly point is minimised
- [ ] C: Fire points with extinguishers and a means of raising the alarm are in position
- [ ] D: There are no records of workers having been trained in the use of fire extinguishers

Answers: 7.16 = D, 7.17 = C, 7.18 = B, 7.19 = C

8.1

Which of these statements about asbestos is true?

- [ ] A: Brown asbestos is safe but blue asbestos is a hazard to health
- [ ] B: White asbestos is safe to use
- [ ] C: All types of asbestos are safe to handle
- [ ] D: All types of asbestos are a hazard to health

8.2

Which symbol means corrosive substance?

- [ ] A: 
- [ ] B: 
- [ ] C: 
- [ ] D:

8.3

Which symbol means toxic substance?

- [ ] A: 
- [ ] B: 
- [ ] C: 
- [ ] D:

8.4

Which symbol means harmful substance?

- [ ] A: 
- [ ] B: 
- [ ] C: 
- [ ] D:

8.5

You find a bottle of chemicals. The bottle does not have a label. What is the first thing you should do?

- [ ] A: Smell the chemical to see what it is
- [ ] B: Put it in a bin to get rid of it
- [ ] C: Put it somewhere safe then report it
- [ ] D: Taste the chemical to see what it is

Answers: 8.1 = D, 8.2 = B, 8.3 = A, 8.4 = C, 8.5 = C

8.6

How can you tell if a product is hazardous?

- [ ] A: By a symbol on the container label
- [ ] B: By the shape of the container
- [ ] C: It will always be in a black container
- [ ] D: It will always be in a cardboard box

8.7

A COSHH assessment tells you how:

- [ ] A: to lift heavy loads and how to protect yourself
- [ ] B: to work safely in confined spaces
- [ ] C: a substance might harm you and how to protect yourself
- [ ] D: noise levels are assessed and how to protect your hearing

8.8

If a substance has this symbol, you must take care because it can:

- [ ] A: burn your skin
- [ ] B: kill you
- [ ] C: catch fire easily
- [ ] D: irritate your skin

8.9

If a substance has this symbol, you must take care because it can:

- [ ] A: kill you
- [ ] B: cause a mild skin rash
- [ ] C: burn your skin
- [ ] D: catch fire easily

8.10

If you breathe in asbestos dust, it can cause:

- [ ] A: aching muscles
- [ ] B: influenza (flu)
- [ ] C: lung disease
- [ ] D: painful joints

Answers: 8.6 = A, 8.7 = C, 8.8 = B, 8.9 = C, 8.10 = C

8.11

The safest way to use a hazardous substance is to:

- [ ] A: get on with the job as quickly as possible
- [ ] B: read your employer's health and safety policy
- [ ] C: read the COSHH assessment and follow the instructions
- [ ] D: ask someone who has already used it

8.12

If you think you have found some asbestos, the first thing you should do is:

- [ ] A: stop work and warn others
- [ ] B: take a sample to the site manager
- [ ] C: put the bits in the bin and carry on with your work
- [ ] D: find the first aider

8.13

When assessing the risk of specifying a substance that you believe to be hazardous you should first:

- [ ] A: review the material safety data sheet
- [ ] B: ensure that safe storage is available on site
- [ ] C: specify that workers must be provided with respiratory equipment
- [ ] D: ensure workers are trained to use respiratory equipment

8.14

Which of these statements apply to asbestos? It is:

- [ ] A: harmful to health
- [ ] B: grey and fibrous
- [ ] C: likely to be found in buildings built between 1950 and 1999
- [ ] D: all the other answers

8.15

If an active asbestos removal enclosure has been set up on site which of the following would indicate that it is operating efficiently?

- [ ] A: Appropriate signage
- [ ] B: Everyone is wearing red suits
- [ ] C: The sides of the enclosure bowing in
- [ ] D: Everyone is wearing respiratory protective equipment

Answers: 8.11 = C, 8.12 = A, 8.13 = A, 8.14 = D, 8.15 = C

8.16

A project involves removing paint from old iron-work. Which of the following would enable the contractor to assess the foreseeable health risk of the work during the tender period?

- [ ] A: Lab-test results of a sample of paint giving its lead content
- [ ] B: The prevailing wind conditions
- [ ] C: Fit testing or respiratory protective equipment
- [ ] D: Tests to determine the average paint thickness

8.17

Flooring is being stuck down by a lone worker, using a liquid adhesive in a small inner room that has no visible means of ventilation. For what reason might you quickly bring this to the attention of the site manager?

- [ ] A: It is illegal for anyone to work on their own
- [ ] B: The work should be carried out under a hot-work station
- [ ] C: Kneeling and working is bad for the worker's back
- [ ] D: The vapours from the adhesive may be a given health hazard without sufficient fresh air

8.18

In a situation where it is not possible to 'design out' the use of a hazardous material, what should be provided to enable the contractor to assess the risk arising from the use of the material?

- [ ] A: A note in the specification
- [ ] B: A material safety data sheet
- [ ] C: An instruction to the planning supervisor
- [ ] D: The designer's risk assessment

Answers: 8.16 = A, 8.17 = D, 8.18 = B

9.1

It is safe to work close to an overhead power line if:

- [ ] A: you do not touch the line for more than 30 seconds
- [ ] B: you use a wooden ladder
- [ ] C: the power is switched off
- [ ] D: it is not raining

9.2

This warning sign means:

- [ ] A: risk of electrocution
- [ ] B: risk of thunder
- [ ] C: electrical appliance
- [ ] D: risk of lighting

9.3

The colour of a 110 volt power cable and connector should be:

- [ ] A: black
- [ ] B: red
- [ ] C: blue
- [ ] D: yellow

9.4

A residual current device (RCD) must be used in conjunction with 230 volt electrical equipment because:

- [ ] A: it lowers the voltage
- [ ] B: it quickly cuts off the power if there is a fault
- [ ] C: it makes the tool run at a safe speed
- [ ] D: it saves energy and lowers costs

9.5

How could you check if the residual current device (RCD) through which a 230 volt hand tool is connected to the supply is working correctly?

- [ ] A: Switch the tool on and off
- [ ] B: Press the test button on the RCD unit
- [ ] C: Switch the power on and off
- [ ] D: Run the tool at top speed to see if it cuts out

Answers: 9.1 = C, 9.2 = A, 9.3 = D, 9.4 = B, 9.5 = B

Electrical Safety & Hand Tools

9.6

Why do building sites use a 110 volt electricity supply instead of the usual 230 volt domestic supply?

- [ ] A: It is cheaper
- [ ] B: It is less likely to kill people
- [ ] C: It moves faster along the cables
- [ ] D: It is safer for the environment

9.7

What is the significance of a yellow plug and a supply cable fitted to an electrical hand tool?

- [ ] A: The tools run off a 110 volt supply
- [ ] B: The tool is waterproof and can be used outdoors in wet conditions
- [ ] C: The tools run off a 240 volt supply and should not be used on site
- [ ] D: The tool has been PAT tested within the past 12 months

9.8

For an enhanced level of personal safety, electrical tools on a site should NOT be:

- [ ] A: 230 volt
- [ ] B: PAT tested
- [ ] C: CE marked
- [ ] D: serviceable

9.9

Someone near you is using a disc cutter to cut concrete blocks. What three immediate hazards are likely to affect you?

- [ ] A: Flying fragments
- [ ] B: Dermatitis
- [ ] C: Dust in the air
- [ ] D: High noise levels
- [ ] E: Skin cancer

9.10

Someone near you is using a laser level. What health hazard is likely to affect you?

- [ ] A: Skin cancer
- [ ] B: None if it is used correctly
- [ ] C: Gradual blindness
- [ ] D: Burning of the skin, similar to sunburn

Answers: 9.6 = B, 9.7 = A, 9.8 = A, 9.9 = A,C,D, 9.10 = B

9.11

Most cutting and grinding machines have guards. What are the two main functions of the guard?

- [ ] A: To stop materials getting onto the blade or wheel
- [ ] B: To give the operator a firm handhold
- [ ] C: To balance the machine
- [ ] D: To stop fragments flying into the air
- [ ] E: To stop the operator coming into contact with the blade or wheel

Answers: 9.11 = D,E

Fire Prevention and Control

10.1

This fire extinguisher contains:

- [ ] A: foam
- [ ] B: carbon dioxide (CO_2)
- [ ] C: water
- [ ] D: dry powder

10.2

A fire assembly point is the place where:

- [ ] A: fire engines must go when they arrive on site
- [ ] B: the fire extinguishers are kept
- [ ] C: people must go when the fire alarm sounds
- [ ] D: the fire started

10.3

This fire extinguisher contains:

- [ ] A: water
- [ ] B: foam
- [ ] C: dry powder
- [ ] D: carbon dioxide (CO_2)

10.4

If you discover a large fire, the first thing you should do is:

- [ ] A: put your tools away
- [ ] B: finish what you are doing if it is safe to do so
- [ ] C: try to put out the fire
- [ ] D: raise the alarm

10.5

If you hear the fire alarm, you should go to:

- [ ] A: the site canteen
- [ ] B: the assembly point
- [ ] C: the site office
- [ ] D: the fire

Answers: 10.1 = C, 10.2 = C, 10.3 = D, 10.4 = D, 10.5 = B

10.6

This extinguisher must **not** be used on:

- [ ] A: electrical fires
- [ ] B: wood fires
- [ ] C: burning furniture
- [ ] D: burning clothes

10.7

If you see 'frost' around the valve on an LPG cylinder, it means:

- [ ] A: the cylinder is nearly empty
- [ ] B: the cylinder is full
- [ ] C: the valve is leaking
- [ ] D: you must lay the cylinder on its side

10.8

If there is a fire, you will need to go to the site assembly point. When would you expect to be told where this is?

- [ ] A: During a visit by the HSE
- [ ] B: During site induction
- [ ] C: By reading your employer's health and safety policy
- [ ] D: Your mates will tell you

10.9

Which two extinguishers are best for putting out oil fires?

- [ ] A:
- [ ] B:
- [ ] C:
- [ ] D:

10.10

This type of fire extinguisher puts out a fire by:

- [ ] A: starving the fire of oxygen
- [ ] B: cooling the burning material
- [ ] C: increasing the oxygen supply
- [ ] D: diluting the oxygen with another gas

Answers: 10.6 = A, 10.7 = C, 10.8 = B, 10.9 = A,C, 10.10 = B

10.11

For safety reasons LPG cylinders used for heating the site cabin must be:

- [ ] A: located outside the cabin
- [ ] B: located inside the cabin but away from the heat source
- [ ] C: connected to the heat source by flexible rubber tubing
- [ ] D: laid on their side

10.12

You would expect to see highly flammable materials being stored:

- [ ] A: under the site manager's desk
- [ ] B: against hoarding furthest away from the site office
- [ ] C: in a secure compound in the open air
- [ ] D: in the timber store

10.13

As a result of design considerations, work will have to be carried out under a hot-work permit. The permit must specify that the work is:

- [ ] A: carried out at a time when the site is otherwise unoccupied
- [ ] B: complete immediately before the end of the working day
- [ ] C: completed in time for any resultant fire to be discovered and dealt with and at least one hour before the site closes
- [ ] D: completed one hour after the permit expires

10.14

Acetylene and oxygen cylinders that are not in use are being stored together outside a meeting room. In the interests of everyone's safety they should be:

- [ ] A: kept on a bottle trolley together
- [ ] B: stored separately and away from site accommodation
- [ ] C: laid down so that they cannot fall over and damage the valves
- [ ] D: stored together but away from site accommodation

10.15

When specifying the requirements for a fuel-oil storage area, you must include:

- [ ] A: water type fire extinguishers
- [ ] B: suitable bunding
- [ ] C: hand-washing facilities
- [ ] D: a porous ground surface to absorb spillage

Answers: 10.11 = A, 10.12 = C, 10.13 = C, 10.14 = B, 10.15 = B

11.1

Which sign means flammable substance?

☐ A:

☐ B:

☐ C:

☐ D:

11.2

This sign means:

☐ A: wear ear protection if you want to

☐ B: you must wear ear protection

☐ C: you must not make a noise

☐ D: caution, noisy machinery

11.3

Fire exit signs are coloured:

☐ A: blue and white

☐ B: red and white

☐ C: green and white

☐ D: red and yellow

11.4

Fire point

This sign tells you where:

☐ A: to go if there is a fire

☐ B: fire extinguishers should be kept

☐ C: a fire will start

☐ D: flammable materials should be kept

11.5

This sign means:

☐ A: press here to sound the fire alarm

☐ B: do not touch

☐ C: wear hand protection

☐ D: press here to switch on the emergency light

Answers: 11.1 = B, 11.2 = B, 11.3 = C, 11.4 = B, 11.5 = A

11.6

This sign means:

- [ ] A: press here to sound the fire alarm
- [ ] B: fire hose reel
- [ ] C: turn key to open
- [ ] D: do not use if there is a fire

11.7

This sign means:

- [ ] A: danger from radiation
- [ ] B: danger from bright lights or lasers
- [ ] C: caution, poor lighting
- [ ] D: you must wear eye protection

11.8

Which sign means 'Warning, laser beams'?

- [ ] A: 
- [ ] B: 
- [ ] C: 
- [ ] D:

11.9

This sign means:

- [ ] A: no access onto the scaffold
- [ ] B: no entry without full Personal Protective Equipment
- [ ] C: no entry for people on foot
- [ ] D: no entry during the day

11.10

Green and white signs mean:

- [ ] A: you **must** do something
- [ ] B: you **must not** do something
- [ ] C: hazard or danger
- [ ] D: safe condition

Answers: 11.6 = B, 11.7 = D, 11.8 = D, 11.9 = C, 11.10 = D

11.11

Blue and white signs mean:

- [ ] A: you **must** do something
- [ ] B: you **must not** do something
- [ ] C: hazard or danger
- [ ] D: safe condition

11.12

Yellow and black signs mean:

- [ ] A: you **must** do something
- [ ] B: you **must not** do something
- [ ] C: hazard or danger
- [ ] D: safe condition

11.13

Red and white signs with a red line mean:

- [ ] A: you **must** do something
- [ ] B: you **must not** do something
- [ ] C: hazard or danger
- [ ] D: safe condition

11.14

This sign means:

- [ ] A: plant operators wanted
- [ ] B: forklift trucks operating
- [ ] C: manual handling not allowed
- [ ] D: storage area

11.15

If you see this sign on a scaffold, you should:

- [ ] A: remove the access ladder
- [ ] B: only work on the first lift
- [ ] C: stay off the scaffold because it is not safe
- [ ] D: only use a Mobile Elevating Work Platform to get on to the scaffold

Answers: 11.11 = A, 11.12 = C, 11.13 = B, 11.14 = B, 11.15 = C

11.16

This sign means:

- [ ] A: you must wear safety boots
- [ ] B: you must wear wellington boots
- [ ] C: caution, slip and trip hazards
- [ ] D: wear safety boots if you want to

11.17

This sign means:

- [ ] A: caution, cold materials
- [ ] B: caution, hot materials
- [ ] C: carry out work using one hand
- [ ] D: you must wear safety gloves

11.18

If you see this sign, you must:

- [ ] A: wear white clothes at night
- [ ] B: wear high visibility clothes
- [ ] C: do nothing, it only applies to managers
- [ ] D: wear wet weather clothes

11.19

A crane has to do a difficult lift. The signaller asks you to help, but you are not trained in plant signals. What should you do?

- [ ] A: Politely refuse because you don't know how to signal
- [ ] B: Start giving signals to the crane driver
- [ ] C: Only help if the signaller really can't manage alone
- [ ] D: Ask the signaller to show you what signals to use

11.20

A truck has to tip materials into a trench. Who should give signals to the truck driver?

- [ ] A: Anyone who is there
- [ ] B: Someone standing in the trench
- [ ] C: Anyone who knows the signals
- [ ] D: Anyone who is trained and competent

Answers: 11.16 = A, 11.17 = D, 11.18 = B, 11.19 = A, 11.20 = D

11.21

This sign means:

- [ ] A: leaking roof
- [ ] B: wear waterproof clothes
- [ ] C: emergency shower
- [ ] D: fire sprinklers

11.22

This sign means:

- [ ] A: do not run
- [ ] B: no escape route
- [ ] C: fire door
- [ ] D: fire escape route

11.23

This sign tells you that a substance is:

- [ ] A: harmful
- [ ] B: toxic
- [ ] C: corrosive
- [ ] D: dangerous to the environment

Answers: 11.21 = C, 11.22 = B, 11.23 = D

Site Transport, Plant and Lifting Operations

12.1

What are the two conditions for being able to operate plant on site?

- [ ] A: You must be competent
- [ ] B: You must be authorised
- [ ] C: You must be over 21 years old
- [ ] D: You must hold a full driving licence
- [ ] E: You must hold a UK passport

12.2

You need to walk past someone using a mobile crane. You should:

- [ ] A: guess what the crane operator will do next and squeeze by
- [ ] B: try to catch the attention of the crane operator
- [ ] C: run to get past the crane quickly
- [ ] D: take another route so that you stay clear of the crane

12.3

You need to walk past a 360° mobile crane. The crane is operating near a wall. What is the main danger?

- [ ] A: The crane could crash into the wall
- [ ] B: You could be crushed if you walk between the crane and the wall
- [ ] C: Whole-body vibration from the crane
- [ ] D: High noise levels from the crane

12.4

You are walking across the site. A large mobile crane reverses across your path. What should you do?

- [ ] A: Help the driver to reverse
- [ ] B: Start to run so that you can pass behind the reversing crane
- [ ] C: Pass close to the front of the crane
- [ ] D: Wait or find another way around the crane

12.5

If you see a dumper being driven too fast, you should:

- [ ] A: keep out of its way and report the matter
- [ ] B: try to catch the dumper and speak to the driver
- [ ] C: report the matter to the police
- [ ] D: do nothing, dumpers are allowed to go above the site speed limit

Answers: 12.1 = A,B, 12.2 = D, 12.3 = B, 12.4 = D, 12.5 = A

12.6

When is site transport allowed to drive along a pedestrian route?

- [ ] A: During meal breaks
- [ ] B: If it is the shortest route
- [ ] C: Only if necessary and if all pedestrians are excluded
- [ ] D: Only if the vehicle has a flashing yellow light

12.7

You see a lorry parking. It has a flat tyre. Why should you tell the driver?

- [ ] A: The lorry will use more fuel
- [ ] B: The lorry will need to travel at a much slower speed
- [ ] C: The lorry is unsafe to drive
- [ ] D: The lorry can only carry small loads

12.8

An excavator has just stopped work. Liquid is dripping and forming a small pool under the back of the machine. What could this mean?

- [ ] A: It is normal for fluids to vent after the machine stops
- [ ] B: The machine is hot so the diesel has expanded and overflowed
- [ ] C: Someone put too much diesel into the machine before it started work
- [ ] D: The machine has a leak and could be unsafe

12.9

You see a driver refuelling an excavator. Most of the diesel is spilling on to the ground. What is the first thing you should do?

- [ ] A: Tell your supervisor the next time you see them
- [ ] B: Tell the driver immediately
- [ ] C: Look for a spillage kit immediately
- [ ] D: Do nothing, the diesel will eventually seep into the ground

12.10

How would you expect a well-organised site to keep pedestrians away from traffic routes?

- [ ] A: The site manager will direct all pedestrians away from traffic routes
- [ ] B: The traffic routes will be shown on the Health and Safety Law poster
- [ ] C: There will be barriers between traffic and pedestrian routes
- [ ] D: There is no need to keep traffic and pedestrians apart

Answers: 12.6 = C, 12.7 = C, 12.8 = D, 12.9 = B, 12.10 = C

12.11

A site vehicle is most likely to injure pedestrians when it is:

- [ ] A: reversing
- [ ] B: lifting materials onto scaffolds
- [ ] C: tipping into an excavation
- [ ] D: digging out footings

12.12

You must not walk behind a lorry when it is reversing because:

- [ ] A: most lorries are not fitted with mirrors
- [ ] B: the driver is unlikely to know you are there
- [ ] C: most lorry drivers aren't very good at reversing
- [ ] D: you will need to run, not walk, to get past it in time

12.13

The quickest way to your work area is through a contractor's vehicle compound. Which way should you go?

- [ ] A: Around the compound if vehicles are moving
- [ ] B: Straight through the compound if no vehicles appear to be moving
- [ ] C: Around the compound every time
- [ ] D: Straight through the compound if no-one is looking

12.14

How would you expect to be told about the site traffic rules?

- [ ] A: During site induction
- [ ] B: By a Health and Safety Executive inspector
- [ ] C: By a note on a notice board
- [ ] D: In a letter sent to your home

12.15

A forklift truck is blocking the way to your work area. It is lifting materials on to a scaffold. What should you do?

- [ ] A: Only walk under the raised load if you are wearing a safety helmet
- [ ] B: Catch the driver's attention and then walk under the raised load
- [ ] C: Start to run so that you are not under the load for very long
- [ ] D: Wait or go around, but never walk under a raised load

Answers: 12.11 = A, 12.12 = B, 12.13 = C, 12.14 = A, 12.15 = D

12.16

A mobile plant operator can let you ride in the machine:

- [ ] A: if you have a long way to go
- [ ] B: if it is raining
- [ ] C: if it is designed to carry passengers
- [ ] D: at any time

12.17

You see a mobile crane lifting a load. The load is about to hit something. What should you do?

- [ ] A: Go and tell the site manager
- [ ] B: Tell the person supervising
- [ ] C: Go and tell the crane driver
- [ ] D: Do nothing and assume everything is under control

12.18

You think a load is about to fall from a moving forklift truck. What should you do?

- [ ] A: Keep clear but try to warn the driver and others in the area
- [ ] B: Run alongside the machine and try to hold on to the load
- [ ] C: Run and tell the site manager
- [ ] D: Sound the nearest fire alarm bell

12.19

The correct procedure for using a tower-crane to off-load a lorry is for:

- [ ] A: lorry drivers to sling the load before the trained slinger/signaler arrives
- [ ] B: anyone to sling the load providing it will not pass over people when on the crane
- [ ] C: a trained slinger/signaler to carry out the off-loading operation
- [ ] D: the crane driver to instruct an operative to sling the load

12.20

Where seat-belts are fitted to mobile plant, they MUST be worn:

- [ ] A: only when travelling on public roads
- [ ] B: only by a front-seat passenger
- [ ] C: at all times
- [ ] D: only if travelling over rough terrain

Answers: 12.16 = C, 12.17 = B, 12.18 = A, 12.19 = C, 12.20 = C

Site Transport, Plant and Lifting Operations

12.21

A visiting professional notes a build-up of diesel fumes in the area of the site that they are visiting. What is the correct course of action they should take? They should:

- [ ] A: turn off the piece of plant that is creating the fumes
- [ ] B: quickly inform the site manager of this hazardous situation
- [ ] C: carry out the visit quickly to minimise exposure
- [ ] D: move out of the affected area at regular intervals to get fresh air

12.22

Which of the following is the most effective way of preventing pedestrians being struck by site vehicles?

- [ ] A: All vehicles must switch on their flashing amber beacon
- [ ] B: Separate access gates and routes for pedestrians and vehicles
- [ ] C: Hi-vis vests being worn when pedestrians walk up the site road
- [ ] D: A wide site road with a good quality surface

12.23

Of the following, which is the best risk control measure with regard to site vehicles reversing?

- [ ] A: Setting a speed limit on site
- [ ] B: Vehicles fitted with reversing bleepers
- [ ] C: A signaler to reverse all vehicles especially on and off site
- [ ] D: All vehicles fitted with CCTV to help them reverse

12.24

All lifting equipment must be:

- [ ] A: brightly coloured, inspected and clearly signed
- [ ] B: regularly maintained, clean and tidy
- [ ] C: logged, inspected, tested, thoroughly examined and marked
- [ ] D: strong enough for the load and always fitted with organisers

Answers: 12.21 = B, 12.22 = B, 12.23 = C, 12.24 = C

12.25

Which of the following represents good site management on the public road approaching a site?

- [ ] A: A place where drivers can park delivery lorries off the road
- [ ] B: Items of plant parked to free up space on site
- [ ] C: Pallets of material stacked on the footpath
- [ ] D: Gates which swing into the road when open

Answer: 12.25 = A

13 Noise and Vibration

13.1

If you wear hearing protection, it will:

- ☐ A: stop you hearing all noise
- ☐ B: reduce noise to an acceptable level
- ☐ C: repair your hearing if it is damaged
- ☐ D: make you hear better

13.2

Noise over a long time can damage your hearing. Can this damage be reversed?

- ☐ A: Yes, with time
- ☐ B: Yes, if you have an operation
- ☐ C: No, the damage is permanent
- ☐ D: Yes, if you change jobs

13.3

If you need to wear hearing protection, you must remember that:

- ☐ A: you have to carry out your own noise assessment
- ☐ B: you have to pay for all hearing protection
- ☐ C: ear plugs don't work
- ☐ D: you may be less aware of what is going on around you

13.4

Two recommended ways to protect your hearing are:

- ☐ A: rolled tissue paper
- ☐ B: cotton wool pads
- ☐ C: ear plugs
- ☐ D: soft cloth pads
- ☐ E: ear defenders

13.5

How can noise affect your health? Give two answers.

- ☐ A: Headaches
- ☐ B: Ear infections
- ☐ C: Hearing loss
- ☐ D: Waxy ears
- ☐ E: Vibration white finger

Answers: 13.1 = B, 13.2 = C, 13.3 = D, 13.4 = C,E, 13.5 = A,C

13.6

You need to wear ear defenders, but an ear pad is missing from one of the shells. What should you do?

- [ ] A: Leave them off and work without any hearing protection
- [ ] B: Put them on and start working with them as they are
- [ ] C: Do not work in noisy areas until they are replaced
- [ ] D: Wrap your handkerchief around the shell and carry on working

13.7

Why is vibration a serious health issue?

- [ ] A: There are no early warning signs
- [ ] B: The long-term effects of vibration are not known
- [ ] C: There is no way that exposure to vibration can be prevented
- [ ] D: Vibration can cause a disabling injury that cannot be cured

13.8

What are three early signs of vibration white finger?

- [ ] A: Temporary loss of feeling in the fingers
- [ ] B: The fingertips turn white
- [ ] C: A skin rash
- [ ] D: Tingling in the fingers
- [ ] E: Blisters

13.9

What is vibration white finger?

- [ ] A: A mild skin rash that will go away
- [ ] B: A serious skin condition that will not clear up
- [ ] C: Severe frostbite
- [ ] D: A sign of damage to your hands and arms that might not go away

13.10

Which of these is most likely to cause vibration white finger?

- [ ] A: Electric hoist
- [ ] B: Hammer drill
- [ ] C: Hammer and chisel
- [ ] D: Battery-powered screwdriver

Answers: 13.6 = C, 13.7 = D, 13.8 = A,B,D, 13.9 = D, 13.10 = B

13.11

After working alongside noisy equipment, you have a 'ringing' sound in your ears. What does this mean?

- [ ] A: Your hearing has been temporarily damaged
- [ ] B: You have also been subjected to vibration
- [ ] C: You are about to go down with the flu
- [ ] D: The noise level was high but acceptable

13.12

Hand-arm vibration can cause:

- [ ] A: skin cancer
- [ ] B: skin irritation, like dermatitis
- [ ] C: blisters on your hands and arms
- [ ] D: damaged blood vessels and nerves in your fingers and hands

13.13

Someone near you is using noisy equipment and you have no hearing protection. What should you do?

- [ ] A: Ask them to stop what they are doing
- [ ] B: Carry on with your work because it is always noisy on site
- [ ] C: Leave the area until you have the correct PPE
- [ ] D: Speak to the other person's supervisor

13.14

At the start of a particular construction operation you become aware that it is generating a high level of noise. It is not possible to shut the operation down. Which of the following actions would you expect to be the site manager's immediate response?

- [ ] A: Arrange for a noise assessment to be carried out
- [ ] B: Make hearing protection available to those people who ask for it
- [ ] C: Issue all people affected with hearing protection as a precaution
- [ ] D: Erect 'Hearing protection zone' signs

Answers: 13.11 = A, 13.12 = D, 13.13 = C, 13.14 = C

14.1

What must happen each time a shift starts work in an excavation?

- [ ] A: Someone must go in and sniff the air to see if it is safe
- [ ] B: A competent person must inspect the excavation
- [ ] C: A supervisor should stay in the excavation for the first hour
- [ ] D: A supervisor should watch from the top for the first hour

14.2

What is the safe way to get into a deep excavation?

- [ ] A: Climb down a ladder
- [ ] B: Use the buried services as steps
- [ ] C: Climb down the shoring
- [ ] D: Go down in an excavator bucket

14.3

You are in a deep trench and start to feel dizzy. What should you do?

- [ ] A: Get out, let your head clear and then go back in again
- [ ] B: Carry on working and hope that the feeling will go away
- [ ] C: Make sure that you and any others get out quickly
- [ ] D: Sit down in the trench and take a rest

14.4

If you need to work in a confined space, one duty of the top man is to:

- [ ] A: tell you how to work safely in confined spaces
- [ ] B: enter the confined space if there is a problem
- [ ] C: start the rescue plan if needed
- [ ] D: supervise the work in the confined space

14.5

Which of these is not a hazard in a confined space?

- [ ] A: Toxic gas
- [ ] B: A lack of carbon dioxide
- [ ] C: A lack of oxygen
- [ ] D: Flammable or explosive gas

Answers: 14.1 = B, 14.2 = A, 14.3 = C, 14.4 = C, 14.5 = B

Excavations and Confined Spaces

14.6

If there is sludge at the bottom of a confined space, you should:

- [ ] A: go in and then step into the sludge to see how deep it is
- [ ] B: throw something into the sludge to see how deep it is
- [ ] C: put on a disposable face-mask before you go in
- [ ] D: have the correct Respiratory Protective Equipment and training before you go in

14.7

Why is methane gas dangerous in confined space? Give two answers.

- [ ] A: It can explode
- [ ] B: It makes you hyperactive
- [ ] C: You will not be able to see because of the dense fumes
- [ ] D: It makes you dehydrated
- [ ] E: You will not have enough oxygen to breathe

14.8

You are in a confined space. If the level of oxygen drops:

- [ ] A: your hearing could be affected
- [ ] B: there is a high risk of fire or explosion
- [ ] C: you could become unconscious
- [ ] D: you might get dehydrated

14.9

You have to work in a confined space. There is no rescue team or rescue plan. What should you do?

- [ ] A: Assume that a rescue team or plan is not necessary and do the job
- [ ] B: Get someone to stand at the opening with a rope
- [ ] C: Do not enter until a rescue plan and team are in place
- [ ] D: Carry out the job in short spells

14.10

You are working in a confined space when you notice the smell of bad eggs. This smell is a sign of:

- [ ] A: hydrogen sulphide
- [ ] B: oxygen
- [ ] C: methane
- [ ] D: carbon dioxide

Answers: 14.6 = D, 14.7 = A,E, 14.8 = C, 14.9 = C, 14.10 = A

14.11

You need to walk through sludge at the bottom of a confined space. Which of these is not a hazard?

- [ ] A: The release of oxygen
- [ ] B: The release of toxic gases
- [ ] C: Slips and trips
- [ ] D: The release of flammable gases

14.12

Guard-rails are placed around the top of an excavation to prevent:

- [ ] A: toxic gases from collecting in the bottom of the trench
- [ ] B: anyone falling into the trench and being injured
- [ ] C: the sides of the trench from collapsing
- [ ] D: rain water running off the ground at the top and into the trench

14.13

You are in a confined space when the gas alarm sounds. You have no Respiratory Protective Equipment, what should you do?

- [ ] A: Switch off the alarm
- [ ] B: Get out of the confined space quickly
- [ ] C: Carry on working but do not use electrical tools
- [ ] D: Carry on working but take plenty of breaks in the fresh air

14.14

You are standing near a deep trench. A lorry backs up to the trench and the engine is left running. What should you do?

- [ ] A: Put on ear defenders to cut out the engine noise
- [ ] B: Ignore the problem, the lorry will soon drive away
- [ ] C: See if there is a toxic gas meter in the trench
- [ ] D: Get everyone out of the trench quickly

14.15

The best way to avoid the potential for someone becoming trapped in an excavation is to:

- [ ] A: eliminate the need for anyone to go into it
- [ ] B: check the contractor's method statement
- [ ] C: review the last excavation inspection record
- [ ] D: go down in a cage suspended from a crane

Answers: 14.11 = A, 14.12 = B, 14.13 = B, 14.14 = D, 14.15 = A

14.16

On well managed sites one effective method of preventing falls into excavations is to identify their location. This is best done by:

- [ ] A: always leaving a pile of soil by them
- [ ] B: showing them on the plan in the site office
- [ ] C: always stand a machine by them
- [ ] D: always placing a suitable barrier around them

14.17

If there is the potential for work to be carried out in a confined space the first consideration should be, can it be:

- [ ] A: undertaken by someone else
- [ ] B: avoided where possible
- [ ] C: managed by limiting the amount of time people are in it
- [ ] D: controlled with radios or mobile phones

Answers: 14.16 = D, 14.17 = B

15.1

What is the purpose of the health and safety file on a construction project?

- [ ] A: To assist people who have to carry out work on the structure in the future
- [ ] B: To assist in the preparation of final accounts for the structure
- [ ] C: To record the health and safety standards of the structure
- [ ] D: To record the accident details

15.2

Which of the following is a fall-arrest system?

- [ ] A: Mobile access equipment
- [ ] B: Scaffold towers
- [ ] C: Mobile elevating work platform
- [ ] D: Safety harness and lanyard

15.3

Which colour identifies the 'live' wire in a 240 volt supply?

- [ ] A: Black
- [ ] B: Brown
- [ ] C: Green
- [ ] D: Yellow

15.4

Which piece of equipment is used with a cable avoidance tool (CAT) to detect cables?

- [ ] A: Compressor
- [ ] B: Signal generator
- [ ] C: Battery
- [ ] D: Gas detector

15.5

In the colour coding of electrical power supplies on site, what voltage does a blue plug represent?

- [ ] A: 50 volts
- [ ] B: 110 volts
- [ ] C: 240 volts
- [ ] D: 415 volts

Answers: 15.1 = A, 15.2 = D, 15.3 = B, 15.4 = B, 15.5 = C

15.6

On the site electrical distribution system, which colour plug indicates a 415 volt supply?

- [ ] A: Yellow
- [ ] B: Blue
- [ ] C: Black
- [ ] D: Red

15.7

Which of the following is a significant hazard when excavating alongside a building or structure?

- [ ] A: Undermining the foundations of the building
- [ ] B: Upsetting the owners of the building
- [ ] C: Excavating too deep in soft ground
- [ ] D: Damage to the surface finish of the building or structure

15.8

What danger is created by excessive oxygen in a confined space?

- [ ] A: Increase in breathing rate of workers
- [ ] B: Increased flammability of combustible materials
- [ ] C: Increased working time inside work area
- [ ] D: False sense of security

15.9

What is the purpose of using a 'permit-to-work' system?

- [ ] A: To ensure that the job is being carried out properly
- [ ] B: To ensure that the job is carried out by the quickest method
- [ ] C: To enable tools and equipment to be properly checked before work starts
- [ ] D: To establish a safe system of work

15.10

An emergency route(s) must be provided on construction sites to ensure:

- [ ] A: safe passage to the ground
- [ ] B: safe passage to open air
- [ ] C: safe passage to a place of safety
- [ ] D: safe passage to the first-aid room

Answers: 15.6 = D, 15.7 = A, 15.8 = B, 15.9 = D, 15.10 = C

15.11

Under the Work at Height Regulations, if part of a system-built scaffold is stopping someone from getting on with their job, the scaffold may be temporarily altered by:

- [ ] A: the person who is being prevented from working
- [ ] B: any site manager
- [ ] C: a trained and competent person
- [ ] D: anyone

15.12

When overhead electric cables cross a construction site, it is recommended that barriers should be erected parallel to the overhead cables at a distance not less than:

- [ ] A: 3 metres
- [ ] B: 4 metres
- [ ] C: 5 metres
- [ ] D: 6 metres

15.13

When is it advisable to take precautions to prevent the fall of materials into an excavation?

- [ ] A: At all times
- [ ] B: When the excavation is 2 or more metres deep
- [ ] C: When more than five people are working in the excavation
- [ ] D: When there is risk from an underground cable or other service

15.14

Sole-boards may be omitted if a scaffold is based on a surface:

- [ ] A: of grass
- [ ] B: of sufficient strength
- [ ] C: of a recently backfilled excavation
- [ ] D: of firm mud

15.15

If a scaffold is not complete, which of the following actions should be taken?

- [ ] A: Make sure the scaffolders complete the scaffold
- [ ] B: Tell all operatives not to use the scaffold
- [ ] C: Use the scaffold with care and a display a warning notice
- [ ] D: Prevent access to the scaffold by unauthorised people

Answers: 15.11 = C, 15.12 = D, 15.13 = A, 15.14 = B, 15.15 = D

15.16

Why is it important that hazards are identified?

- [ ] A: They have the potential to cause harm
- [ ] B: They must all be eliminated before work can start
- [ ] C: They must all be notified to the Health and Safety Executive
- [ ] D: They have to be written on the Health and Safety Law poster

15.17

Under the requirements of the Work at Height Regulations, the minimum width of a working platform must be:

- [ ] A: 3 boards wide
- [ ] B: suitable for the job in hand
- [ ] C: 2 boards wide
- [ ] D: any width

15.18

Following a scaffold inspection under the Work at Height Regulations, how soon must a report be given to the person on whose behalf the inspection was made?

- [ ] A: Within 2 hours
- [ ] B: Within 6 hours
- [ ] C: Within 12 hours
- [ ] D: Within 24 hours

15.19

If precautions are taken to prevent people and items falling, scaffold guard-rails may be temporarily removed provided that:

- [ ] A: they are replaced as soon as practicable
- [ ] B: the scaffolding does not become overloaded
- [ ] C: the scaffolding does not begin to sway
- [ ] D: the intermediate guard-rail is left in position

15.20

The Work at Height Regulations require a working platform to be inspected:

- [ ] A: after an accident
- [ ] B: every day
- [ ] C: fortnightly
- [ ] D: before first use and then every seven days afterwards

Answers: 15.16 = A, 15.17 = B, 15.18 = D, 15.19 = A, 15.20 = D

15.21

An assessment has been carried out under the Control of Substances Hazardous to Health Regulations. To which of the following should the risks and control measures be explained?

- A: All employees on site
- B: The operatives using the substance
- C: The person in charge of the stores
- D: The accounts department

15.22

The Work at Height Regulations require inspections of scaffolding to be carried out by:

- A: the site manager
- B: the scaffolder
- C: the safety adviser
- D: a competent person

15.23

For a ladder, what is the maximum vertical height that may be climbed before an intermediate landing place is required?

- A: 7.5 metres
- B: 8.0 metres
- C: 8.5 metres
- D: 9.0 metres

15.24

On a scaffold, the minimum height of the main guard-rail must be:

- A: 875mm
- B: 910mm
- C: 950mm
- D: 1000mm

15.25

On a scaffold, the unprotected gap between any guard-rail, toe-board, barrier or other similar means of protection should not exceed:

- A: 400mm
- B: 470mm
- C: 500mm
- D: 600mm

15.26

When setting up a fuel storage tank on site, a spillage bund must have a minimum capacity of:

- A: the contents of the tank + 10%
- B: the contents of the tank + 15%
- C: the contents of the tank + 20%
- D: the contents of the tank + 25%

Answers: 15.21 = B, 15.22 = D, 15.23 = D, 15.24 = C, 15.25 = B, 15.26 = A

15.27

In the context of a risk assessment, what does the term 'risk' mean?

- [ ] A: Something with the potential to cause injury
- [ ] B: An unsafe act or condition
- [ ] C: The likelihood that harm from a particular hazard will be realised
- [ ] D: Any work activity that can be described as dangerous

15.28

Which of the following precautions should be taken to prevent a dumper from falling into an excavation when tipping material into it?

- [ ] A: Keep 5 metres away from the excavation
- [ ] B: Provide a stop block appropriate to the vehicle's wheel size
- [ ] C: Judge the distance carefully
- [ ] D: Approach the excavation in reverse gear

15.29

The number of people who may be carried in a passenger hoist on site must be:

- [ ] A: displayed in the site canteen
- [ ] B: displayed on a legible notice within the cage of the hoist
- [ ] C: given in the company safety policy
- [ ] D: given to the operator of the hoist

15.30

A Health and Safety Inspector may visit your site:

- [ ] A: if 7 days' notice is given
- [ ] B: if any length of notice is given in writing
- [ ] C: at any time without notice
- [ ] D: only if invited by a senior member of staff

15.31

The Health and Safety at Work Act and any regulations made under that Act are:

- [ ] A: advisory to companies and individuals
- [ ] B: legally binding
- [ ] C: good practical advice for the employer to follow
- [ ] D: not compulsory, but should be complied with if convenient

15.32

Under the Construction (Design and Management) Regulations, which of the following must the principal contractor ensure is specifically provided before allowing any demolition work to commence?

- [ ] A: A construction phase safety plan
- [ ] B: A written method statement
- [ ] C: A generic risk assessment
- [ ] D: A pre-tender health and safety plan

Answers: 15.27 = C, 15.28 = B, 15.29 = B, 15.30 = C, 15.31 = B, 15.32 = B

15.33

The minimum level of first-aid cover required at any workplace is an appointed person. Which of the following would you expect the appointed person to do?

- [ ] A: Provide **most** of the care normally carried out by a first-aider
- [ ] B: Provide **all** the care normally provided by a first-aider
- [ ] C: Contact the emergency services and direct them to the scene of an accident
- [ ] D: Only apply splints to broken bones

15.34

The advantage of using safety nets rather than harness and lanyard is that safety nets:

- [ ] A: do not need inspecting
- [ ] B: are cheaper
- [ ] C: provide collective fall protection
- [ ] D: can be rigged by anyone

15.35

What should you do for the safety of private motorists if transport leaving your site is likely to deposit mud on the public road?

- [ ] A: Have someone in the road to slow down the traffic
- [ ] B: Employ an on-site method of washing the wheels of site transport
- [ ] C: Employ a mechanical road sweeper
- [ ] D: Have someone hosing-down the mud in the road

15.36

What should you do if you notice that operatives working above a safety net are dropping off-cuts of material and other debris into the net?

- [ ] A: Nothing, as at least it is all collecting in one place
- [ ] B: Ensure that the net is cleared of debris weekly
- [ ] C: Have the net cleared and ensure it is not allowed to happen again
- [ ] D: Ensure that the net is cleared of debris daily

Answers: 15.33 = C, 15.34 = C, 15.35 = B, 15.36 = C

15.37

What should be included in a safety method statement for working at height? Give three answers.

- [ ] A: The cost of the job and time it will take
- [ ] B: The sequence of operations and the equipment to be used
- [ ] C: How much insurance cover will be required
- [ ] D: How falls are to be prevented
- [ ] E: Who will supervise the job on site

15.38

When putting people to work above public areas, your first consideration should be:

- [ ] A: to minimise the number of people below at any one time
- [ ] B: to prevent complaints from the public
- [ ] C: to let the public know what you are doing
- [ ] D: to prevent anything falling on to people below

15.39

A competent person must routinely inspect a scaffold:

- [ ] A: after it is erected and at intervals not exceeding 7 days
- [ ] B: only after it has been erected
- [ ] C: after it is erected and then at monthly intervals
- [ ] D: after it is erected and then at intervals not exceeding 10 days

15.40

Ideally, a safety net should be rigged:

- [ ] A: immediately below where you are working
- [ ] B: 2 metres below where you are working
- [ ] C: 6 metres below where you are working
- [ ] D: at any height below the working position

15.41

Someone wearing a safety harness has a fall. What is the main danger of leaving them suspended for too long?

- [ ] A: The anchorage point may fail
- [ ] B: They may try to climb back up the structure and fall again
- [ ] C: They will suffer severe discomfort and may lose consciousness
- [ ] D: It will discourage other people from working at height

Answers: 15.37 = B,D,E, 15.38 = D, 15.39 = A, 15.40 = A, 15.41 = C

15.42

Edge protection must be designed to:

- [ ] A: make access to the roof easier
- [ ] B: secure tools and materials close to the edge
- [ ] C: stop rainwater running off the roof onto workers below
- [ ] D: prevent people and materials falling

15.43

When should guard-rails be fitted to a working platform?

- [ ] A: If it is possible to fall 2 metres
- [ ] B: At any height if a fall could result in an injury
- [ ] C: If it is possible to fall 3 metres
- [ ] D: Only if materials are being stored on the working platform

15.44

The Beaufort Scale is important when you have people working at height because it measures:

- [ ] A: air temperature
- [ ] B: the load-bearing capacity of a flat roof
- [ ] C: wind speed
- [ ] D: the load-bearing capacity of a scaffold

15.45

A design feature of some air bags used for fall arrest is a controlled leak rate. If you are using these, the inflation pump must:

- [ ] A: be electrically powered
- [ ] B: be switched off from time to time to avoid over-inflation
- [ ] C: run all the time while work is carried out at height
- [ ] D: be switched off when the air bags are full

15.46

Why is it dangerous to use inflatable air bags that are too big for the area to be protected?

- [ ] A: They will exert a sideways pressure on anything that is containing them
- [ ] B: The pressure in the bags will cause them to burst
- [ ] C: The inflation pump will become overloaded
- [ ] D: They will not fully inflate

Answers: 15.42 = D, 15.43 = B, 15.44 = C, 15.45 = C, 15.46 = A

15.47

Who should you inform if someone reports to you that they have work-related hand-arm vibration syndrome?

- [ ] A: The Health and Safety Executive
- [ ] B: The local Health Authority
- [ ] C: A coroner
- [ ] D: The nearest hospital

15.48

How should cylinders containing LPG be stored on site?

- [ ] A: In a locked cellar with clear warning signs
- [ ] B: In a locked external compound at least 3 metres from any oxygen cylinders
- [ ] C: As close to the point of use as possible
- [ ] D: Covered by a tarpaulin to shield the compressed cylinder from sunlight

15.49

How should access be controlled, if you have people working in a riser shaft?

- [ ] A: By a site security operative
- [ ] B: By those who are working in it
- [ ] C: By the main contractor
- [ ] D: By a Permit to Work system

15.50

Before allowing a lifting operation to be carried out, you must ensure that the sequence of operations to enable a lift to be carried out safely is confirmed in:

- [ ] A: verbal instructions
- [ ] B: a method statement
- [ ] C: a radio telephone message
- [ ] D: a notice in the canteen

15.51

Where should liquefied petroleum gas (LPG) cylinders be positioned when supplying an appliance in a site cabin?

- [ ] A: Inside the site cabin in a locked cupboard
- [ ] B: Under the cabin
- [ ] C: Inside the cabin next to the appliance
- [ ] D: Outside the cabin

Answers: 15.47 = A, 15.48 = B, 15.49 = D, 15.50 = B, 15.51 = D

15.52

Welding is about to start on your site. What should be provided to prevent passers-by from getting arc-eye:

- [ ] A: warning signs
- [ ] B: screens
- [ ] C: PPE
- [ ] D: nothing

15.53

Why may young people be more at risk of having accidents?

- [ ] A: Legislation does not apply to anyone under 18 years of age
- [ ] B: They are usually left to work alone to gain experience
- [ ] C: They are inexperienced and may not recognise danger
- [ ] D: There is no legal duty to provide them with PPE

15.54

What is your least reliable source of information when assessing the level of vibration from a powered percussive hand tool?

- [ ] A: In-use vibration measurement of the tool
- [ ] B: Vibration figures taken from the tool manufacturer's hand book
- [ ] C: Your own judgment based upon observation
- [ ] D: Vibration data from the HSE's master list

15.55

To whom should the CDM co-ordinator pass the health and safety file on completion of the construction project?

- [ ] A: The Association for Project Safety
- [ ] B: The client
- [ ] C: The Health and Safety Executive
- [ ] D: The designer

Answers: 15.52 = B, 15.53 = C, 15.54 = C, 15.55 = B

15.56

When planning possible work in a confined space, what should be the first consideration?

- [ ] A: How long the job will take
- [ ] B: To avoid the need for anyone to enter the space
- [ ] C: How many operatives will be required
- [ ] D: Personal protective equipment

15.57

What is the best way for a responsible person to make sure that all who are doing a job have fully understood a method statement?

- [ ] A: Put the method statements in a labelled spring-binder in the office
- [ ] B: Explain the method statement to those doing the job
- [ ] C: Make sure that those doing the job have read the method statement
- [ ] D: Display the method statement on a notice board in the office

15.58

Someone has agreed to become a first-aider and you have been told to make the appropriate arrangements. What course of action should you take?

- [ ] A: Give the volunteer a first-aid manual to read
- [ ] B: Ask a qualified first-aider from another company to brief the volunteer
- [ ] C: Show the volunteer where the first-aid kit is and let them take it from there
- [ ] D: Ensure the volunteer attends an appropriate first-aid course

Answers: 15.56 = B, 15.57 = B, 15.58 = D

15.59

What should you do if a Health and Safety Inspector arrives on site and wants to see your Site Diary following an accident?

- [ ] A: Hand the diary over
- [ ] B: Tear any pages out that you feel may be incriminating before handing it over
- [ ] C: Flatly refuse to hand over the diary
- [ ] D: Refuse to hand over the diary until you have consulted with your Senior Management

15.60

From a safety point of view, which of the following should be considered first when deciding on the number and location of access and egress points to a site?

- [ ] A: Parking for senior manager's cars
- [ ] B: Access for the emergency services
- [ ] C: Access for heavy vehicles
- [ ] D: Site security

15.61

Which one of the following directly controls the way works are undertaken on site?

- [ ] A: The Principal Contractors' Health and Safety Policy Statement
- [ ] B: The local Health and Safety Executive Inspector
- [ ] C: The Principal Contractors' Health and Safety Plan
- [ ] D: The Health and Safety at Work etc Act 1974

15.62

In order to manage the safety of site visitors which of the following documents must the Principal Contractor keep under review?

- [ ] A: The Health and Safety File
- [ ] B: Designers' risk assessments
- [ ] C: Project programme
- [ ] D: The construction phase Health and Safety Plan

Answers: 15.59 = A, 15.60 = B, 15.61 = C, 15.62 = D

15.63

Where must you be able to find the name and address of the client, CDM co-ordinator and principal contractor?

- [ ] A: The construction phase health and safety plan
- [ ] B: The HSE Form 10
- [ ] C: The site notice board
- [ ] D: The accident book

15.64

The practical way for the Principal Contractor to ensure co-operation from sub-contractors is to:

- [ ] A: monitor their works, explain their legal duties and help them comply
- [ ] B: haul them over the coals when they do something wrong
- [ ] C: withhold payments when they do not perform satisfactorily
- [ ] D: wait to make comments at the next progress meeting

15.65

Having completed their risk assessment, what is the usual method used by contractors to control an on-going, hazardous activity?

- [ ] A: By banning it from site
- [ ] B: By ensuring that the foreman always does it
- [ ] C: By standing over the operative while the work is done
- [ ] D: By having a Permit system

15.66

On a contaminated land remediation project which of the following would you expect to be in place to avoid contamination of the surrounding area?

- [ ] A: Warning signs that state that visitors are excluded from the site
- [ ] B: Overalls for all visitors
- [ ] C: Adequate provision for vehicle wheel washing
- [ ] D: Respiratory protective equipment for all visitors

Answers: 15.63 = B, 15.64 = A, 15.65 = D, 15.66 = C

15.67

On a contaminated land remediation project what should be provided to help workers protect their own health?

- [ ] A: Lockable skips
- [ ] B: Plenty of fresh drinking water
- [ ] C: Good signage of contaminated areas
- [ ] D: Good welfare facilities

15.68

Which one of the following would you expect sub-contractors to primarily focus on to manage the risks arising from their work?

- [ ] A: The construction phase health and safety plan
- [ ] B: ConstructionSkills publication; Construction Site Safety (GE 700)
- [ ] C: Task-specific risk assessments and method statements
- [ ] D: The HSE Form 10

15.69

On what basis would you expect the topics for toolbox talks to be selected?

- [ ] A: They are picked at random from the list of toolbox talks
- [ ] B: So that the topic relates to work that is being carried out at that time
- [ ] C: The client selects the topic for each talk
- [ ] D: In strict order so that each talk is given at least once a year

15.70

A planned task which involves significant risk should only be undertaken by:

- [ ] A: a competent person
- [ ] B: whoever can do it most quickly
- [ ] C: a person who has got the time
- [ ] D: someone who understands the risks

Answers: 15.67 = D, 15.68 = C, 15.69 = B, 15.70 = A

15.71

You are aware that a particular activity is being carried out under a permit to work system. This tells you that:

- [ ] A: an HSE inspector is visiting the site
- [ ] B: the HSE has authorised the job to proceed
- [ ] C: particular hazards have been identified for which additional control measures were necessary
- [ ] D: a minimum of three people are necessary for the job to be carried out safely

15.72

Which of the following provides a good first impression of how well a site is currently being run?

- [ ] A: How tidy it is
- [ ] B: What the contractor says in the monthly site meeting
- [ ] C: What last month's health and safety inspection report says
- [ ] D: How often toolbox talks are given

15.73

Which of the following would you not expect to contribute significantly to the practical management of health and safety on site?

- [ ] A: Sub-contractors' risk assessments and method statements
- [ ] B: Sub-contractors' certificate of Employers' Liability Insurance
- [ ] C: The principles of the Construction (Design and Management) Regulations
- [ ] D: The construction phase health and safety plan

15.74

What is the main benefit and purpose of toolbox talks?

- [ ] A: They are something for the operatives to do when it is raining
- [ ] B: They are a way of checking on the presence of site staff
- [ ] C: They update personnel on how to approach a particular issue
- [ ] D: They replace the need for induction training for operatives

Answers: 15.71 = C, 15.72 = A, 15.73 = B, 15.74 = C

15.75

The standards of health and safety on a project site have noticeably declined. As the responsible professional what is the first thing you should do to find out about the contractor's attitude to health and safety?

- [ ] A: Review their health and safety inspection reports
- [ ] B: Go out on site and look
- [ ] C: Start a dialogue with the site manager
- [ ] D: Call the contractor's safety department

15.76

What is likely to be the most effective way of keeping children off construction sites?

- [ ] A: Put up 'Keep Out' posters
- [ ] B: Close and lock all doors and gates in the site security barrier
- [ ] C: Visits to local schools
- [ ] D: Send a flier to local households telling them to keep their children off site

Answers: 15.75 = C, 15.76 = B

Demolition

16.1

If there are any doubts as to a building's stability, a demolition contractor should consult:

- [ ] A: another demolition contractor
- [ ] B: a structural engineer
- [ ] C: an HSE Factory Inspector
- [ ] D: the company safety advisor

16.2

What should you do if you discover underground services not previously identified?

- [ ] A: Fill in the hole and say nothing to anyone
- [ ] B: Stop work until the situation has been resolved
- [ ] C: Cut the pipe or cable to see if it's live
- [ ] D: Get the machine driver to dig it out

16.3

What is the most common source of high levels of lead in the blood of operatives doing demolition work?

- [ ] A: Stripping lead sheeting
- [ ] B: Cutting lead-covered cable
- [ ] C: Cold cutting fuel tanks
- [ ] D: Hot cutting coated steel

16.4

On site, what is the minimum distance that oxygen should be stored away from propane, butane or other gases?

- [ ] A: 1 metre
- [ ] B: 2 metres
- [ ] C: 3 metres
- [ ] D: 4 metres

16.5

What type of fire extinguisher should not be provided where petrol is being stored?

- [ ] A: Foam
- [ ] B: Water
- [ ] C: Dry powder
- [ ] D: Carbon dioxide

Answers: 16.1 = B, 16.2 = B, 16.3 = D, 16.4 = C, 16.5 = B

16.6

What action should you take if you discover unlabelled drums or containers on site?

- [ ] A: Put them in the nearest waste skip
- [ ] B: Ignore them. They will get flattened during the demolition
- [ ] C: Stop work until they have been safely dealt with
- [ ] D: Open them and smell the contents

16.7

Which is the safest method of demolishing brick or internal walls by hand?

- [ ] A: Undercut the wall at ground level
- [ ] B: Work across in even courses from the ceiling down
- [ ] C: Work from the doorway at the full height
- [ ] D: Cut down at corners and collapse in sections

16.8

Who should be consulted before demolition is carried out near to overhead cables?

- [ ] A: The Health and Safety Executive
- [ ] B: The Fire Service
- [ ] C: The electricity supply company
- [ ] D: The land owner

16.9

Where would you find the intended method of controlling identified hazards on a demolition project?

- [ ] A: The structural plans
- [ ] B: The risk assessments
- [ ] C: The site welfare plans
- [ ] D: The Health and Safety Law poster

Answers: 16.6 = C, 16.7 = B, 16.8 = C, 16.9 = B

16.10

Before entering large open-topped tanks, what is the most important thing you should obtain?

- [ ] A: A ladder for easy access
- [ ] B: A valid permit to work
- [ ] C: An operative to keep watch over you
- [ ] D: A gas meter to detect any gas

16.11

After exposure to lead, what precautions should you take before eating or drinking?

- [ ] A: Wash your hands and face
- [ ] B: Do not smoke
- [ ] C: Change out of dirty clothes
- [ ] D: Brush your teeth

16.12

When hinge-cutting a steel building or structure for a 'controlled collapse', which should be the last cuts?

- [ ] A: Front leading row top cuts
- [ ] B: Front leading row bottom cuts
- [ ] C: Back-row top cuts
- [ ] D: Back-row bottom cuts

16.13

What type of fire extinguisher should you not use in confined spaces?

- [ ] A: Water
- [ ] B: Carbon dioxide
- [ ] C: Dry powder
- [ ] D: Foam

16.14

Before carrying out the demolition cutting of fuel tanks what should be obtained?

- [ ] A: A gas free certificate
- [ ] B: An isolation certificate
- [ ] C: A risk assessment
- [ ] D: A COSHH assessment

Answers: 16.10 = B, 16.11 = A, 16.12 = D, 16.13 = B, 16.14 = A

16.15

How long is a gas free certificate issued for?

- [ ] A: One week
- [ ] B: One month
- [ ] C: One day
- [ ] D: One hour

16.16

What do the letters SWL stand for?

- [ ] A: Satisfactory working limit
- [ ] B: Safe working level
- [ ] C: Satisfactory weight limit
- [ ] D: Safe working load

16.17

Which of the following is true as regards to the safe working load of a piece of equipment?

- [ ] A: It must never be exceeded
- [ ] B: It is a guide figure that may be exceeded slightly
- [ ] C: It may be exceeded by 10%
- [ ] D: It gives half the maximum weight to be lifted

16.18

What should be clearly marked on all lifting gear?

- [ ] A: Date of manufacture
- [ ] B: Name of maker
- [ ] C: Date next due for test
- [ ] D: Safe working load

16.19

Lifting accessories must be thoroughly examined every:

- [ ] A: 3 months
- [ ] B: 6 months
- [ ] C: 14 months
- [ ] D: 18 months

Answers: 16.15 = C, 16.16 = D, 16.17 = A, 16.18 = D, 16.19 = B

16.20

Plant and equipment needs to be inspected and the details recorded by operators:

- [ ] A: daily at the beginning of each shift
- [ ] B: weekly
- [ ] C: monthly
- [ ] D: every 3 months

16.21

What is the importance of having ROPS fitted to some mobile plant?

- [ ] A: It ensures that the pressure of the tyres is correct
- [ ] B: It protects the operator if the machine rolls over
- [ ] C: It prevents over-pressurisation of the hydraulic system
- [ ] D: It prevents unauthorised passengers being carried out

16.22

Where do you find information about daily checks required for mobile plant?

- [ ] A: On the stickers attached to the machine
- [ ] B: In the manufacturer's handbook
- [ ] C: In the supplier's information
- [ ] D: Any or all of the other answers

16.23

What action should be taken if a wire rope sling is defective?

- [ ] A: Do not use it and make sure that no one else can
- [ ] B: Only use it for up to half its safe working load
- [ ] C: Put it to one side to wait for repair
- [ ] D: Only use it for small lifts under 1 tonne

16.24

When must head and tail lights be used on mobile plant?

- [ ] A: Only if using the same traffic route as private cars
- [ ] B: In all conditions of poor visibility
- [ ] C: When operated by a trainee
- [ ] D: Only if crossing pedestrian routes

Answers: 16.20 = B, 16.21 = B, 16.22 = D, 16.23 = A, 16.24 = B

16.25

With regard to mobile plant, what safety feature is provided by FOPS?

- [ ] A: The speed is limited when tracking over hard surfaces
- [ ] B: The machine stops automatically if the operator lets go of the controls
- [ ] C: The operator is protected from falling materials
- [ ] D: The reach is limited when working near to live overhead cables

16.26

Which one of the following is an effective way of ensuring good standards of health and safety on a demolition project?

- [ ] A: Checking the contractor's method statement
- [ ] B: Selecting a competent demolition contractor
- [ ] C: Ensuring operatives use personal protective equipment as necessary
- [ ] D: All of the other answers

University of South Wales
Prifysgol De Cymru

Answers: 16.25 = C, 16.26 = D

17 Plumbing or Gas

17.1

The legionella bacteria that cause Legionnaire's disease are most likely to be found in which of the following?

- [ ] A: A boiler operating at a temperature of 80° centigrade
- [ ] B: A shower hose outlet
- [ ] C: A cold water storage containing water at 10° centigrade
- [ ] D: A WC toilet pan

17.2

How are legionella bacteria passed on to humans?

- [ ] A: Through fine water droplets such as sprays or mists
- [ ] B: By drinking dirty water
- [ ] C: Through contact with the skin
- [ ] D: From other people when they sneeze

17.3

The reason for carrying out temporary continuity bonding before removing and replacing sections of metallic pipework is to:

- [ ] A: provide a continuous earth for the pipework installation
- [ ] B: prevent any chance of blowing a fuse
- [ ] C: maintain the live supply to the electrical circuit
- [ ] D: prevent any chance of corrosion to the pipework

17.4

Which of the following statements is true?

- [ ] A: Both propane and butane are heavier than air
- [ ] B: Butane is heavier than air while propane is lighter than air
- [ ] C: Propane is heavier than air while butane is lighter than air
- [ ] D: Both propane and butane are lighter than air

17.5

Apart from the cylinders used in gas-powered forklift trucks, liquefied petroleum gas cylinders should never be placed on their sides during use because:

- [ ] A: it would give a faulty reading on the contents gauge, resulting in flashback
- [ ] B: air could be drawn into the cylinder, creating a dangerous mixture of gases
- [ ] C: the liquid gas would be at too low a level to allow the torch to burn correctly
- [ ] D: the liquid gas could be drawn from the cylinder, creating a safety hazard

Answers: 17.1 = B, 17.2 = A, 17.3 = A, 17.4 = A, 17.5 = D

17.6

What is the preferred method of checking for leaks when assembling liquefied petroleum gas equipment before use?

- [ ] A: Test with a lighted match
- [ ] B: Sniff the connections to detect the smell of gas
- [ ] C: Listen for escaping gas
- [ ] D: Apply leak detection fluid to the connections

17.7

What is the colour of propane gas cylinders?

- [ ] A: Black
- [ ] B: Maroon
- [ ] C: Red/Orange
- [ ] D: Blue

17.8

You arrive at a job which involves using ladder access to the roof. You notice the ladder has been painted. You should:

- [ ] A: only use the ladder if it is made of metal
- [ ] B: only use the ladder if it is made of wood
- [ ] C: only use the ladder if wearing rubber-soled boots to prevent slipping
- [ ] D: not use the ladder, and report the matter to your supervisor

17.9

Which of the following makes it essential to take great care when handling oxygen cylinders?

- [ ] A: They contain highly flammable compressed gas
- [ ] B: They contain highly flammable liquid gas
- [ ] C: They are filled to extremely high pressure
- [ ] D: They contain poisonous gas

17.10

What is the colour of an acetylene cylinder?

- [ ] A: Orange
- [ ] B: Black
- [ ] C: Green
- [ ] D: Maroon

Answers: 17.6 = D, 17.7 = C, 17.8 = D, 17.9 = C, 17.10 = D

17.11

Which of the following is the safest place to store oxyacetylene gas welding bottles when they are not in use?

- [ ] A: Outside in a special storage compound
- [ ] B: In company vehicles
- [ ] C: Inside the building in a locked cupboard
- [ ] D: In the immediate work area, ready for use the next day

17.12

In plumbing work, what part of the body could suffer long-term damage when hand bending copper pipe using an internal spring?

- [ ] A: Elbows
- [ ] B: Hands
- [ ] C: Back
- [ ] D: Knees

17.13

Which of the following is most likely to result in those who work with sheet lead having raised levels of lead in their blood?

- [ ] A: By them not using the correct respirator
- [ ] B: By not washing their hands before eating
- [ ] C: By not changing out of their work clothes
- [ ] D: By them not wearing safety goggles

17.14

Why is it important to know the difference between propane and butane equipment?

- [ ] A: Propane equipment operates at higher pressure
- [ ] B: Propane equipment operates at lower pressure
- [ ] C: Propane equipment is cheaper
- [ ] D: Propane equipment can be used with smaller, easy-to-handle cylinders

17.15

What item of personal protective equipment, from the following list, should be used when someone is oxyacetylene welding?

- [ ] A: Ear defenders
- [ ] B: Clear goggles
- [ ] C: Green-tinted goggles
- [ ] D: Dust mask

Answers: 17.11 = A, 17.12 = D, 17.13 = B, 17.14 = A, 17.15 = C

17.16

When observing oxyacetylene welding equipment, the bottles should be:

- [ ] A: laid on their side
- [ ] B: stood upright
- [ ] C: stood upside down
- [ ] D: angled at 45°

17.17

When working in an area where fibreglass roof insulation is being handled, in addition to safety boots and helmet, which of the following items of personal protective equipment (PPE) should be worn?

- [ ] A: Gloves, face mask and eye protection
- [ ] B: Rubber apron, eye protection and ear defenders
- [ ] C: Ear defenders, face mask and boots
- [ ] D: Barrier cream, eye protection and face mask

Answers: 17.16 = B, 17.17 = A

18 Highway Works

18.1

What are two effects of under-inflated tyres on the operation of a machine?

- [ ] A: It decreases the operating speed of the engine
- [ ] B: It leads to instability of the machine
- [ ] C: It causes increased tyre wear
- [ ] D: It decreases tyre wear
- [ ] E: It increases the operating speed of the engine

18.2

Which of the following is true as regards to the safe working load of lifting equipment such as a cherry picker, lorry loader or excavator?

- [ ] A: It must never be exceeded
- [ ] B: It is a guide figure that may be exceeded slightly
- [ ] C: It may be exceeded by 10% only
- [ ] D: It gives half the maximum weight to be lifted

18.3

Which of the following checks should the operator of a mobile elevating work platform, for example a cherry picker, carry out before using it?

- [ ] A: Check that a seat belt is provided for the operator
- [ ] B: Check that a roll-over cage is fitted
- [ ] C: Drain the hydraulic system
- [ ] D: Check that emergency systems operate correctly

18.4

In which of the following circumstances would it not be safe to use a cherry picker for working at height?

- [ ] A: When a roll-over cage is not fitted
- [ ] B: When the ground is uneven and sloping
- [ ] C: When weather protection is not fitted
- [ ] D: When the operator is clipped to an anchorage point in the basket

Answers: 18.1 = B,C, 18.2 = A, 18.3 = D, 18.4 = B

18.5

When providing portable traffic signals on roads used by cyclists and horse riders, what action should you take?

- [ ] A: Locate the signals at bends in the road
- [ ] B: Allow more time for slow-moving traffic by increasing the 'all red' phase of the signals
- [ ] C: Operate the signals manually
- [ ] D: Use 'stop/go' boards only

18.6

What is the purpose of an on-site risk assessment?

- [ ] A: To ensure there is no risk of traffic build-up due to the works in progress
- [ ] B: To identify hazards and risks in order to ensure a safe system of work
- [ ] C: To ensure that the work can be carried out in reasonable safety
- [ ] D: To protect the employer from prosecution

18.7

When working on a dual carriageway with a 60mph speed limit, unless in the working space, what is the minimum standard of high-visibility clothing that must be worn?

- [ ] A: Reflective waistcoat
- [ ] B: Reflective long-sleeved jacket
- [ ] C: None
- [ ] D: Reflective sash

18.8

Why should temporary signing be removed when works are complete?

- [ ] A: To get traffic flowing
- [ ] B: It is a legal requirement
- [ ] C: To allow the road to be opened fully
- [ ] D: To reuse signs on new job

18.9

When should installed signs and guarding equipment be inspected?

- [ ] A: After it has been used
- [ ] B: Once a week
- [ ] C: Before being used
- [ ] D: Regularly and at least once every day

Answers: 18.5 = B, 18.6 = B, 18.7 = B, 18.8 = B, 18.9 = D

18.10

What two site conditions must prevail so that the minimum traffic management can be used?

- [ ] A: Traffic should be heavy
- [ ] B: Visibility is good
- [ ] C: Double parking will be required
- [ ] D: Rush hour
- [ ] E: Period of low risk

18.11

What traffic management is required when carrying out a maintenance job on a motorway?

- [ ] A: The same as would be required on a single carriageway
- [ ] B: A flashing beacon and a 'keep left/right' sign
- [ ] C: A scheme installed by a registered traffic management contractor
- [ ] D: Ten 1-metre high cones and a 1-metre high 'men working' sign

18.12

What is the minimum traffic management required when carrying out a short term minor maintenance job in a quiet, low-speed side road?

- [ ] A: A flashing amber beacon and a 'keep left/right' arrow
- [ ] B: The same as required for a road excavation
- [ ] C: Five cones and a blue arrow
- [ ] D: Temporary traffic light

18.13

Mobile works are being carried out by day. A single vehicle is being used. What must be conspicuously displayed on or at the rear of the vehicle?

- [ ] A: Road narrows (left or right)
- [ ] B: A specific task warning sign (for example, gully cleaning)
- [ ] C: A 'keep left/right' arrow
- [ ] D: A 'roadworks ahead' sign

18.14

Some work activities move along the carriageway, such as sweeping, verge mowing and road lining. What is the maximum distance between the 'roadworks ahead' signs?

- [ ] A: 2 miles
- [ ] B: 1 mile
- [ ] C: Half a mile
- [ ] D: Quarter of a mile

Answers: 18.10 = B,E, 18.11 = C, 18.12 = A, 18.13 = C, 18.14 = B

18.15

What action is required when a vehicle fitted with a direction arrow is travelling from site to site?

- A: Point the direction arrow up
- B: Travel slowly from site to site
- C: Point the direction arrow down
- D: Cover or remove the direction arrow

18.16

Signs placed on footways must be located so that they:

- A: block the footway
- B: can be read by site personnel
- C: do not create a hazard for pedestrians
- D: can be easily removed

18.17

What should you do if drivers approaching roadworks cannot see the advance signs clearly because of poor visibility or obstructions caused by road features?

- A: Place additional signs in advance of the works
- B: Extend the safety zones
- C: Extend the sideways clearance
- D: Lengthen the lead-in taper

18.18

What action is required where passing traffic may block the view of signs?

- A: Signs must be larger
- B: Signs must be duplicated on both sides of the road
- C: Signs must be placed higher
- D: Additional signs must be placed in advance of the works

18.19

In which two places would you find information on the distances for setting out the signs in advance of the works under different road conditions?

- A: In the Traffic Signs Manual (Chapter 8)
- B: In the 'Pink Book'
- C: On the back of the sign
- D: In the specification for highway works
- E: The code of Practice ('Red Book')

Answers: 18.15 = D, 18.16 = C, 18.17 = A, 18.18 = B, 18.19 = A,E

18.20

Signs, lights and guarding equipment must be properly secured:

- [ ] A: with sacks containing fine granular material set at a low level
- [ ] B: by roping them to concrete blocks or kerb stones
- [ ] C: to prevent them being stolen
- [ ] D: by iron weights suspended from the frame by frame chains or other strong material

18.21

Which is not an approved means of controlling traffic at roadworks?

- [ ] A: Priority signs
- [ ] B: Police supervision
- [ ] C: Hand signals by operatives
- [ ] D: A give-and-take system

18.22

What action is required where it is not possible to maintain the correct safety zone?

- [ ] A: Barrier off the working space
- [ ] B: Place additional advance signing
- [ ] C: Use extra cones on the lead-in taper
- [ ] D: Stop work and consult your supervisor

18.23

On a dual carriageway, a vehicle driven by a member of the public enters the coned-off area. What action do you take?

- [ ] A: Remove a cone and direct the driver back on to the live carriageway
- [ ] B: Ignore them
- [ ] C: Shout and wave them off site
- [ ] D: Assist them to leave the site safely via the nearest designated exit

18.24

What is the purpose of the 'safety zone'?

- [ ] A: To indicate the works area
- [ ] B: To protect you from the traffic and the traffic from you
- [ ] C: To allow extra working space in an emergency
- [ ] D: To give a safe route around the working area

18.25

When should you switch on the amber flashing beacon fitted to your vehicle?

- [ ] A: At all times
- [ ] B: When travelling to and from the depot
- [ ] C: When the vehicle is being used as a works vehicle
- [ ] D: Only in poor visibility

Answers: 18.20 = A, 18.21 = C, 18.22 = D, 18.23 = D, 18.24 = B, 18.25 = C

18.26

When driving into a site works access on a motorway, what must you do approximately 200 metres before the access?

- [ ] A: Switch on the vehicle hazard lights
- [ ] B: Switch on flashing amber beacon
- [ ] C: Switch on the headlights
- [ ] D: Switch on the flashing amber beacon and the appropriate indicator

18.27

Lifting equipment for carrying persons, for example a cherry picker, must be thoroughly examined by a competent person every:

- [ ] A: 12 months
- [ ] B: 24 months
- [ ] C: 18 months
- [ ] D: 6 months

18.28

From a safety point of view, diesel must not be used to prevent asphalt sticking to the bed of lorries because:

- [ ] A: it will create a slipping hazard
- [ ] B: it will corrode the bed of the lorry
- [ ] C: it will create a fire hazard
- [ ] D: it will react with the asphalt, creating explosive fumes

18.29

When kerbing works are being carried out, which method should be used for getting kerbs off the vehicle?

- [ ] A: Lift them off manually using the correct technique
- [ ] B: Push them off the back
- [ ] C: Use mechanical means, such as a JCB fitted with a grab
- [ ] D: Ask your workmate to give you a hand

Answers: 18.26 = D, 18.27 = D, 18.28 = A, 18.29 = C

18.30

Why is it necessary to wear high-visibility clothing when working on roads?

- [ ] A: So road users and plant operators can see you
- [ ] B: So that your colleagues can see you
- [ ] C: Because you were told to
- [ ] D: Because it will keep you warm

18.31

In which of the following circumstances can someone enter the safety zone?

- [ ] A: To store unused plant
- [ ] B: To maintain cones and signs
- [ ] C: To park site vehicles
- [ ] D: To store materials

18.32

If you are working after dark, is mobile plant exempt from the requirement to show lights?

- [ ] A: Yes, on all occasions
- [ ] B: Yes, if authorised by the site manager
- [ ] C: Only if they are not fitted to the machine as standard
- [ ] D: Not in any circumstances

Answers: 18.30 = A, 18.31 = B, 18.32 = D

Professionally Qualified Person 19

Professionally Qualified Person

19.1

Who is responsible for reporting any unsafe conditions on site?

- [ ] A: The site manager only
- [ ] B: The client
- [ ] C: HSE inspectors
- [ ] D: Everyone on site

19.2

A risk assessment tells you:

- [ ] A: how to report accidents
- [ ] B: the site working hours
- [ ] C: how to do the job safely
- [ ] D: where the first-aid box is kept

19.3

The Health and Safety at Work Act places legal duties on:

- [ ] A: employers only
- [ ] B: operatives only
- [ ] C: all people at work
- [ ] D: self-employed people only

19.4

Why do you need to know the health and safety regulations that deal with your type of work?

- [ ] A: They tell you how to write risk assessments
- [ ] B: They explain how health and safety is managed on your site
- [ ] C: They tell you when HSE inspections will take place
- [ ] D: They place legal duties on you

19.5

Who is responsible for managing health and safety on construction sites?

- [ ] A: The police
- [ ] B: The HSE
- [ ] C: The client
- [ ] D: The site manager

19.6

You will often hear the word hazard mentioned. What does it mean?

- [ ] A: Anything at work that can cause harm
- [ ] B: The site accident rate
- [ ] C: A type of barrier or machine guard
- [ ] D: All of the other answers

Answers: 19.1 = D, 19.2 = C, 19.3 = C, 19.4 = D, 19.5 = D, 19.6 = A

19.7

A whole site has been issued with a Prohibition Notice. What does this mean?

- [ ] A: The site manager should be on site before work starts
- [ ] B: You must check with the HSE before starting work
- [ ] C: You must not use any tools or machinery
- [ ] D: Work must stop on site until the safety problem is rectified

19.8

Why is the Health and Safety at Work Act important to anyone at work? Give two answers.

- [ ] A: It tells you which parts of the site are dangerous
- [ ] B: It must be learned before starting work
- [ ] C: It requires all employers to provide a safe place to work
- [ ] D: It tells you how to do your job
- [ ] E: It puts legal duties on employees with regard to their acts or omissions

19.9

It is important for those at work to see their employer's health and safety policy because it tells them:

- [ ] A: how to do their job safely
- [ ] B: how to write risk assessments
- [ ] C: how health and safety is managed within their organisation
- [ ] D: how to use tools and equipment safely

19.10

When must you record an accident in the accident book?

- [ ] A: If you are injured in any way
- [ ] B: Only if you have to be off work
- [ ] C: Only if you have suffered a broken bone
- [ ] D: Only if you have to go to hospital

19.11

If someone is injured at work, who should record it in the accident book?

- [ ] A: The site manager, and no one else
- [ ] B: The injured person, or someone acting for them
- [ ] C: The first-aider, and no one else
- [ ] D: Someone from the HSE

Answers: 19.7 = D, 19.8 = C,E, 19.9 = C, 19.10 = A, 19.11 = B

19.12

Why is it important to report all accidents?

- [ ] A: It might stop them happening again
- [ ] B: Some types of accident have to be reported to the HSE
- [ ] C: Details have to be entered in the accident book
- [ ] D: All of the other answers

19.13

Why is it important to report all near miss accidents?

- [ ] A: The HSE need to know about everything that happens on site
- [ ] B: To find someone to blame
- [ ] C: You might want to claim compensation
- [ ] D: To learn from them and stop them happening again

19.14

You can help prevent accidents by:

- [ ] A: reporting unsafe working conditions
- [ ] B: becoming a first-aider
- [ ] C: knowing where the first-aid kit is kept
- [ ] D: knowing how to get help quickly

19.15

When are staff on site most likely to have an accident?

- [ ] A: In the morning
- [ ] B: In the afternoon
- [ ] C: During the summer months
- [ ] D: When they first start on site

19.16

Historically, which type of accident kills most construction workers?

- [ ] A: Falling from height
- [ ] B: Contact with electricity
- [ ] C: Being run over by site transport
- [ ] D: Being hit by a falling object

19.17

Which of these helps everyone work safely on site?

- [ ] A: Site induction
- [ ] B: Toolbox talks
- [ ] C: Risk assessments and method statements
- [ ] D: All of the other answers

Answers: 19.12 = D, 19.13 = D, 19.14 = A, 19.15 = D, 19.16 = A, 19.17 = D

19.18

Two kinds of animal can carry a disease called Leptospirosis in their urine. Which two?

- [ ] A: Cat
- [ ] B: Sheep
- [ ] C: Rat
- [ ] D: Rabbit
- [ ] E: Cow

19.19

Look at these statements about illegal drugs in the workplace. Which one is true?

- [ ] A: Users of illegal drugs are a danger to everyone on site
- [ ] B: People who take illegal drugs work better and faster
- [ ] C: People who take illegal drugs take fewer days off work
- [ ] D: Taking illegal drugs is a personal choice so other people shouldn't worry about it

19.20

If you get a hazardous substance on your hands, it can pass from your hands to your mouth when you eat. Give two ways to stop this.

- [ ] A: Wear protective gloves while you are working
- [ ] B: Wash your hands before eating
- [ ] C: Put barrier cream on your hands before eating
- [ ] D: Wear protective gloves then turn them inside-out before eating
- [ ] E: Wash your work gloves then put them on again before eating

19.21

The early signs of Weil's disease (Leptospirosis) can be easily confused with:

- [ ] A: dermatitis
- [ ] B: diabetes
- [ ] C: hayfever
- [ ] D: influenza (flu)

Answers: 19.18 = C,E, 19.19 = A, 19.20 = A,B, 19.21 = D

19.22

It is your first day on site. You find that there is nowhere for you to wash your hands. What should you do?

- ☐ A: Wait until you get home then wash them
- ☐ B: Go to a local café or pub and use the washbasin in their toilet
- ☐ C: Speak to the site manager about the problem
- ☐ D: Bring your own bottle of water the next day

19.23

What sort of rest area should be provided for operatives on site?

- ☐ A: A covered area
- ☐ B: A covered area and some chairs
- ☐ C: A covered area, tables and chairs, and something to heat water
- ☐ D: Nothing, contractors don't have to provide rest areas

19.24

What is the minimum that should be provided on site for washing hands?

- ☐ A: Nothing, there is no need to provide washing facilities
- ☐ B: Running hot water and electric hand-dryers
- ☐ C: A cold water standpipe and paper towels
- ☐ D: Hot and cold water (or warm water), soap and a way to dry hands

19.25

Why should operatives not just rely on barrier cream to protect their skin from harmful substances, because:

- ☐ A: it costs too much to use every day
- ☐ B: many harmful substances go straight through it
- ☐ C: it is difficult to wash off
- ☐ D: it can irritate your skin

19.26

Occupational asthma is a disease that can end someone's working life. It affects their:

- ☐ A: hearing
- ☐ B: joints
- ☐ C: skin
- ☐ D: breathing

Answers: 19.22 = C, 19.23 = C, 19.24 = D, 19.25 = B, 19.26 = D

19.27

The site toilets do not flush. What should you do?

- [ ] A: Try not to use the toilets while you are at work
- [ ] B: Tell the site manager about the problem and ensure that they are fixed
- [ ] C: Try to fix the fault yourself
- [ ] D: Ask a plumber to fix the fault

19.28

Under the regulations for manual handling, all employees must:

- [ ] A: wear back-support belts when lifting anything
- [ ] B: make a list of all the heavy things they have to carry
- [ ] C: lift any size of load once the risk assessment has been done
- [ ] D: make full use of their employer's safe systems of work

19.29

An employee of your organisation has to lift loads as part of their work. What must your employer do?

- [ ] A: Make sure they are supervised during the lifting operation
- [ ] B: Carry out a risk assessment of the task
- [ ] C: Nothing, it is part of some work operations to lift loads
- [ ] D: Watch while the load is lifted

19.30

Someone has to move a load while they are sitting, not standing. How much can they lift safely?

- [ ] A: Less than usual
- [ ] B: The usual amount
- [ ] C: Twice the usual amount
- [ ] D: Three times the usual amount

19.31

It is safe to cross a fragile roof if you:

- [ ] A: walk along the line of bolts
- [ ] B: can see fragile roof signs
- [ ] C: don't walk on any plastic panels
- [ ] D: use crawling boards

Answers: 19.27 = B, 19.28 = D, 19.29 = B, 19.30 = A, 19.31 = D

19.32

You are working on a flat roof. What is the best way to stop yourself falling over the edge?

- [ ] A: Put a large warning sign at the edge of the roof
- [ ] B: Ask someone to watch you and shout when you get too close to the edge
- [ ] C: Protect the edge with a guard-rail and toe-board
- [ ] D: Use red and white tape to mark the edge

19.33

A ladder should not be painted because:

- [ ] A: the paint will make it slippery to use
- [ ] B: the paint may hide any damaged parts
- [ ] C: the paint could damage the metal parts of the ladder
- [ ] D: it will need regular re-painting

19.34

You need to use a ladder to reach a work platform. What should be the slope or angle of the ladder?

- [ ] A: 45°
- [ ] B: 60°
- [ ] C: 75°
- [ ] D: 85°

19.35

You are working above water and there is a risk of falling. Which two items of PPE do you need?

- [ ] A: Wellington boots
- [ ] B: Harness and lanyard
- [ ] C: Life jacket
- [ ] D: Waterproof jacket
- [ ] E: Waterproof trousers

19.36

You need to use a ladder to get to a scaffold platform. Which of these statements is true?

- [ ] A: It must be tied and extend about five rungs above the platform
- [ ] B: All broken rungs must be clearly marked
- [ ] C: It must be wedged at the bottom to stop it slipping
- [ ] D: Two people must be on the ladder at all times

Answers: 19.32 = C, 19.33 = B, 19.34 = C, 19.35 = B,C, 19.36 = A

19.37

What is the best way to stop people falling through fragile roof panels?

- [ ] A: Tell everyone where the panels are
- [ ] B: Cover the panels with something that can take the weight of a person
- [ ] C: Cover the panels with netting
- [ ] D: Mark the panels with red and white tape

19.38

You need to use a mobile tower scaffold. The wheel brakes do not work. What should you do?

- [ ] A: Use some wood to wedge the wheels and stop them moving
- [ ] B: Do not use the tower
- [ ] C: Only use the tower if the floor is level
- [ ] D: Get someone to hold the tower while you use it

19.39

When you climb a ladder, you must:

- [ ] A: have three points of contact with the ladder at all times
- [ ] B: have two points of contact with the ladder at all times
- [ ] C: use a safety harness
- [ ] D: have two people on the ladder at all times

19.40

What does this sign mean?

- [ ] A: Do not run on the roof
- [ ] B: Slippery when wet
- [ ] C: Fragile roof
- [ ] D: Load-bearing roof

19.41

When materials are stored on a working platform, the site manager must make sure:

- [ ] A: the materials are secure, even in windy weather
- [ ] B: the platform can take the weight of the materials
- [ ] C: the materials do not make the platform unsafe for others
- [ ] D: all of the other answers

19.42

You need to reach the working platform of a mobile tower scaffold. What is the right way to do this?

- [ ] A: Climb up the tower frame on the outside of the tower
- [ ] B: Lean a ladder against the tower and climb up that
- [ ] C: Climb up the ladder built into the tower
- [ ] D: Jump from the rigid structure on which you are working

Answers: 19.37 = B, 19.38 = B, 19.39 = A, 19.40 = C, 19.41 = D, 19.42 = C

19.43

A mobile tower scaffold must not be used on:

- A: soft or uneven ground
- B: a paved patio
- C: an asphalt road
- D: a smooth concrete path

19.44

You are working at height when you could fall from:

- A: the first lift of a scaffold or higher
- B: 2 metres above the ground or higher
- C: any height that would cause an injury if you fell
- D: 3 metres above the ground or higher

19.45

You find a ladder that is damaged. What should you do?

- A: Don't let anyone use it and inform the site manager about the damage
- B: Don't use it and report the damage at the end of the day
- C: Ask someone to try and mend the damage
- D: Use the ladder if you can avoid the damaged part

19.46

When can a ladder be used as a place of work?

- A: If it is long enough
- B: If a ladder is available
- C: If other people do not need to use it for access
- D: If you are doing light work for a short time

19.47

You must wear head protection on site at all times unless you are:

- A: self-employed
- B: working alone
- C: in a safe area, like the site office
- D: working in very hot weather

19.48

An employer must supply PPE:

- A: twice a year
- B: if employees pay for it
- C: if it is in the contract
- D: if it is needed to provide protection

Answers: 19.43 = A, 19.44 = C, 19.45 = A, 19.46 = D, 19.47 = C, 19.48 = D

19.49

Do employees have to pay for any PPE they need?

- [ ] A: Yes, they must pay for all of it
- [ ] B: Only to replace lost or damaged PPE
- [ ] C: Yes, but they only have to pay half the cost
- [ ] D: No, the employer must pay for it

19.50

If you drop your safety helmet from height on to a hard surface, you should:

- [ ] A: have any cracks repaired then carry on wearing it
- [ ] B: make sure there are no cracks then carry on wearing it
- [ ] C: work without a safety helmet until you can get a new one
- [ ] D: stop work and get a new safety helmet

19.51

One of your employees needs to wear a full body harness. They have never used one before. What should you do?

- [ ] A: Provide them with information, expert advice and training
- [ ] B: Ask someone wearing a similar harness to show them what to do
- [ ] C: Ask them to work it out for themselves
- [ ] D: Ask them to read the instruction book

19.52

Look at these statements about anti-vibration gloves. Which one is true?

- [ ] A: They might not provide protection against vibration
- [ ] B: They cut out all hand-arm vibration
- [ ] C: They only work against low frequency vibration
- [ ] D: They give the most protection if they are worn over other gloves

19.53

A first-aid box should not contain:

- [ ] A: bandages
- [ ] B: plasters
- [ ] C: safety pins
- [ ] D: pain killers

Answers: 19.49 = D, 19.50 = D, 19.51 = A, 19.52 = A, 19.53 = D

19.54

Someone collapses with stomach pain. There is no first-aider on site. What should you do?

- A: Get them to sit down
- B: Get someone to call the emergency services
- C: Get them to lie down in the recovery position
- D: Give them some pain killers

19.55

If someone falls and is knocked unconscious, you should:

- A: turn them over so they are lying on their back
- B: send for medical help
- C: slap their face to wake them up
- D: give mouth-to-mouth resuscitation

19.56

This sign means:

- A: wear eye protection
- B: eye-wash station
- C: risk of splashing
- D: shower block

19.57

This sign means:

- A: one-way system
- B: public right of way
- C: assembly point
- D: site transport route

19.58

What is the one thing a first-aider cannot do?

- A: Give mouth-to-mouth resuscitation
- B: Stop any bleeding
- C: Give medicines without authorisation
- D: Treat casualties if they are unconscious

19.59

Do those in charge of sites have to provide a first aid box?

- A: Yes, every site must have one
- B: **Only** if more than 50 people work on site
- C: **Only** if more than 25 people work on site
- D: No, there is no legal duty to provide

Answers: 19.54 = B, 19.55 = B, 19.56 = B, 19.57 = C, 19.58 = C, 19.59 = A

19.60

Where should you be able to find the emergency telephone number for a site? Give two answers.

- [ ] A: From the site induction
- [ ] B: From the site notice boards
- [ ] C: Ask the HSE
- [ ] D: Ask the local hospital
- [ ] E: Look in the BT telephone directory

19.61

If there is an emergency while you are on site, you should first:

- [ ] A: leave the site and go back to your office
- [ ] B: phone your office
- [ ] C: follow the site emergency procedure
- [ ] D: phone the police

19.62

The COSHH Regulations deal with:

- [ ] A: the safe use of tools and equipment
- [ ] B: the safe use of lifting equipment
- [ ] C: the safe use of hazardous substances
- [ ] D: safe working at height

19.63

This symbol tells you a substance is:

- [ ] A: harmful
- [ ] B: toxic
- [ ] C: corrosive
- [ ] D: an irritant

19.64

This symbol tells you a substance is:

- [ ] A: harmful
- [ ] B: toxic
- [ ] C: corrosive
- [ ] D: an irritant

19.65

If a substance has this symbol, why must you take care? Give two answers.

- [ ] A: It can catch fire easily
- [ ] B: It can irritate your skin
- [ ] C: It can harm your health
- [ ] D: It can kill you
- [ ] E: It can burn your skin

Answers: 19.60 = A,B, 19.61 = C, 19.62 = C, 19.63 = B, 19.64 = C, 19.65 = B,C

19.66

Which of these does not cause skin problems?

- [ ] A: Asbestos
- [ ] B: Bitumens
- [ ] C: Epoxy resins
- [ ] D: Solvents

19.67

Which of these will give you health and safety information about a hazardous substance?

- [ ] A: The site diary
- [ ] B: The delivery note
- [ ] C: The COSHH assessment
- [ ] D: The accident book

19.68

How should hazardous waste be disposed of?

- [ ] A: It should be put in any skip on site
- [ ] B: In accordance with the site rules
- [ ] C: It should be buried on site
- [ ] D: It should be taken to the nearest local authority waste tip

19.69

On building sites, the recommended safe voltage for electrical equipment is:

- [ ] A: 12 volts
- [ ] B: 24 volts
- [ ] C: 110 volts

19.70

The PAT test label on a power tool tells you:

- [ ] A: when the next safety check is due
- [ ] B: when the tool was made
- [ ] C: who tested the tool before it left the factory
- [ ] D: its earth-loop impedance

19.71

How does this type of extinguisher put out fires?

- [ ] A: It gets rid of the heat
- [ ] B: It keeps out oxygen
- [ ] C: It removes the fuel
- [ ] D: It makes the fire wet

Answers: 19.66 = A, 19.67 = C, 19.68 = B, 19.69 = C, 19.70 = A, 19.71 = B

19.72

To put out an oil fire, you must **not** use:

A:

B:

C:

D:

19.73

When a carbon dioxide (CO_2) fire extinguisher is used, the nozzle gets:

A: very cold

B: very hot

C: warm

D: very heavy

19.74

All fires need **heat, fuel** and:

A: oxygen

B: carbon dioxide

C: argon

D: nitrogen

19.75

This extinguisher can be used to put out:

A: burning oil

B: electrical fires

C: wood fires

D: burning petrol

19.76

This extinguisher must **not** be used on:

A: electrical fires

B: wood fires

C: burning oil

D: burning petrol

19.77

Which **two** extinguishers can be used on electrical fires?

A:

B:

C:

D:

Answers: 19.72 = D, 19.73 = A, 19.74 = A, 19.75 = C, 19.76 = A, 19.77 = A,D

19.78

Work is taking place in a corridor that is a fire escape route. You must ensure that:

- [ ] A: tools and equipment do not block the route
- [ ] B: all doors into the corridor are locked
- [ ] C: only spark-proof tools are used
- [ ] D: all fire escape signs are removed before work starts

19.79

When you walk across the site, what is the best way to avoid an accident with mobile plant?

- [ ] A: Keep to the pedestrian routes
- [ ] B: Ride on the plant
- [ ] C: Get the attention of the driver before you get too close
- [ ] D: Wear high visibility clothing

19.80

Which of these would you not expect to see if site transport is well organised?

- [ ] A: Speed limits
- [ ] B: Barriers to keep pedestrians away from mobile plant and vehicles
- [ ] C: Pedestrians and mobile plant using the same routes
- [ ] D: One-way systems

19.81

Noise can damage your hearing. What is an early sign of this?

- [ ] A: There are no early signs
- [ ] B: Temporary deafness
- [ ] C: A skin rash around the ears
- [ ] D: Ear infections

19.82

If you have to enter a 'hearing protection zone', you must:

- [ ] A: not make any noise
- [ ] B: wear hearing protection at all times
- [ ] C: take hearing protection with you in case you need to use it
- [ ] D: wear hearing protection if the noise gets too loud for you

19.83

Noise may be a problem if you have to shout to be clearly heard by someone who is standing:

- [ ] A: 2 metres away
- [ ] B: 4 metres away
- [ ] C: 5 metres away
- [ ] D: 6 metres away

Answers: 19.78 = A, 19.79 = A, 19.80 = C, 19.81 = B, 19.82 = B, 19.83 = A

19.84

Operatives are less likely to suffer from hand-arm vibration if they are:

- [ ] A: very cold but dry
- [ ] B: cold and wet
- [ ] C: warm and dry
- [ ] D: very wet but warm

19.85

An excavation must be supported if:

- [ ] A: it is more than 5 metres deep
- [ ] B: it is more than 12 metres deep
- [ ] C: there is a risk of the sides falling in
- [ ] D: any buried services cross the excavation

19.86

Which of these is the most accurate way to locate buried services?

- [ ] A: Cable plans
- [ ] B: Trial holes
- [ ] C: Survey drawings
- [ ] D: Architect's drawings

19.87

Before work starts in a confined space, how should the air be checked?

- [ ] A: Someone should go in and sniff the air
- [ ] B: The air should be tested with a meter
- [ ] C: Someone should look around to see if there is toxic gas
- [ ] D: The air should be tested with a match to see if it stays alight

19.88

You are looking at an excavation. If you see the side supports move, you should:

- [ ] A: keep watching to see if they move again
- [ ] B: make sure that everyone working in the excavation gets out quickly
- [ ] C: do nothing as the sides move all the time
- [ ] D: move to another part of the excavation

Answers: 19.84 = C, 19.85 = C, 19.86 = B, 19.87 = B, 19.88 = B

19.89

Work in a confined space usually needs three safety documents – a risk assessment, a method statement and:

- [ ] A: a Permit to Work
- [ ] B: an up-to-date staff handbook
- [ ] C: a written contract for the work
- [ ] D: a company health and safety policy

19.90

Where a project is notifiable under the Construction (Design and Management) Regulations, what must be in place before construction work begins?

- [ ] A: Construction project health and safety file
- [ ] B: Construction phase health and safety plan
- [ ] C: Construction project plan
- [ ] D: Construction contract agreement

19.91

What form can be used to inform the HSE of those projects that are notifiable under the Construction (Design and Management) Regulations?

- [ ] A: Form F9 (Rev)
- [ ] B: Form F10 (Rev)
- [ ] C: Form 11 (Rev)
- [ ] D: Form 12 (Rev)

19.92

Where a project is notifiable under the Construction (Design and Management) Regulations, who is responsible for ensuring notification to the Health and Safety Executive of the project?

- [ ] A: Client
- [ ] B: Designer
- [ ] C: CDM co-ordinator
- [ ] D: Principal contractor

19.93

If a new build project is notifiable under the Construction (Design and Management) Regulations, the client must ensure that construction does not start until:

- [ ] A: the construction phase health and safety plan is in place
- [ ] B: a site manager has been employed to take charge
- [ ] C: the Health and Safety Executive has given permission
- [ ] D: the health and safety file is in place

Answers: 19.89 = A, 19.90 = B, 19.91 = B, 19.92 = C, 19.93 = A

19.94

During the construction phase, the CDM co-ordinator has responsibilities for which two activities under the Construction (Design and Management) Regulations?

- [ ] A: Ensuring co-operation between designers and the principal contractor
- [ ] B: Appointing a competent and adequately resourced designer
- [ ] C: Deciding which construction processes are to be used
- [ ] D: Ensuring that relevant pre-construction information is identified and collected
- [ ] E: The on-going monitoring site safety throughout the construction phase

19.95

If, as a result of an accident at work, an employee is absent from work for more than three days, how soon must the Health and Safety Executive be notified?

- [ ] A: Within 3 days
- [ ] B: Within 5 days
- [ ] C: Within 7 days
- [ ] D: Within 10 days

19.96

If there is a fatal accident on site, when must the Health and Safety Executive be informed?

- [ ] A: Immediately
- [ ] B: Within 5 days
- [ ] C: Within 7 days
- [ ] D: Within 10 days

19.97

Following a reportable dangerous occurrence, when must the Health and Safety Executive be informed?

- [ ] A: Within 1 day
- [ ] B: Within 5 days
- [ ] C: Within 10 days
- [ ] D: Immediately

19.98

Employers must prevent exposure of their employees to substances hazardous to health. Where this is not reasonably practicable, which of the following should be done first?

- [ ] A: Provide instruction, training and supervision
- [ ] B: Carry out proper health surveillance
- [ ] C: Minimise risk and control exposure
- [ ] D: Monitor the exposure of employees in the workplace

Answers: 19.94 = A,D, 19.95 = D, 19.96 = A, 19.97 = D, 19.98 = C

19.99

The monitoring and controlling of health and safety procedures can be proactive or reactive. Reactive monitoring means:

- ☐ A: ensuring that staff are doing the work that they have been instructed to do
- ☐ B: looking at incidents after the event so that remedial action can be taken
- ☐ C: making sure that worksheets are up to date
- ☐ D: keeping a hazard book for use by all staff

19.100

In deciding which control measures to take, following a risk assessment which has revealed a risk, what measure should you always consider first?

- ☐ A: Make sure personal protective equipment is available
- ☐ B: Adapt the work to the individual
- ☐ C: Give priority to those measures which protect the whole workforce
- ☐ D: Avoid the risk altogether if possible

19.101

The monitoring and controlling of health and safety procedures can be either proactive or reactive. Proactive monitoring means:

- ☐ A: ensuring that staff always do the work that they have been instructed to do safely
- ☐ B: deciding how to prevent accidents similar to those that have already occurred
- ☐ C: looking at the work to be done, what could go wrong and how it could be done safely
- ☐ D: checking that all staff read and understand all health and safety notices

19.102

In considering what measures to take to protect people against risks to their health and safety, personal protective equipment should always be regarded as:

- ☐ A: the first line of defence
- ☐ B: the only practical measure
- ☐ C: the best way to tackle the job
- ☐ D: the last resort

Answers: 19.99 = B, 19.100 = D, 19.101 = C, 19.102 = D

19.103

Where a project is notifiable under the Construction (Design and Management) Regulations, who is responsible for preparing the construction phase health and safety plan?

- A: The principal contractor
- B: The client
- C: A contractor tendering for the project
- D: The CDM co-ordinator

19.104

Apart from work for domestic clients, under the Construction (Design and Management) Regulations, in which two of the following situations must the Health and Safety Executive be notified of a project?

- A: Where the work will last more than 30 days or more than 500 person-days
- B: Where the building and construction work will last more than 300 person-days
- C: Where the building and construction work is expected to last more than six months
- D: Where there is more than one building to be erected
- E: When the work will take place outside normal hours

19.105

Under the Construction (Design and Management) Regulations, which of the following is responsible for initially making pre-construction information available?

- A: The CDM co-ordinator
- B: The principal contractor
- C: The client
- D: The client's agent

19.106

The Construction (Design and Management) Regulations require a supported excavation to be inspected:

- A: every 7 days
- B: at the start of every shift
- C: once a month
- D: when it is more than 2 metres deep

19.107

Before starting any construction work lasting more than 30 days, or 500 person-days, which of the following must be done?

- A: The local authority must be informed on a Form F9
- B: The health and safety file must be handed to the client
- C: The client must prepare a pre-tender health and safety plan
- D: The Health and Safety Executive must be notified

Answers: 19.103 = A, 19.104 = A,C, 19.105 = C, 19.106 = B, 19.107 = D

19.108

An employer has to prepare a written health and safety policy if:

- [ ] A: they employ 5 people or more
- [ ] B: they employ more than 3 people
- [ ] C: they employ a safety officer
- [ ] D: the work is going to last more than 30 days

19.109

The new-style accident book must now be used because it:

- [ ] A: contains the personal details of everyone on site
- [ ] B: can only be completed by a Site Manager or Supervisor
- [ ] C: complies with the requirements of the Data Protection Act
- [ ] D: can only be kept in an electronic format

19.110

If a prohibition notice is issued by an inspector of the Health and Safety Executive or local authority:

- [ ] A: work can continue, provided that a risk assessment is carried out
- [ ] B: the work that is subject to the notice must cease
- [ ] C: the work can continue if extra safety precautions are taken
- [ ] D: the work in hand can be completed, but no new works started

19.111

The Management of Health and Safety at Work Regulations 1999 require risk assessments to be made:

- [ ] A: for all work activities
- [ ] B: when there is a danger of someone getting hurt
- [ ] C: when more than five people are employed
- [ ] D: where an accident has happened previously

19.112

Where a project is notifiable under the requirements of the Construction (Design and Management) Regulations, what has to be displayed on a construction site?

- [ ] A: Notice of application to erect hoarding
- [ ] B: Notice of the Health and Safety Commission's address
- [ ] C: Form F10 (Rev) or a notice carrying specified information
- [ ] D: A statement by the client

Answers: 19.108 = A, 19.109 = C, 19.110 = B, 19.111 = A, 19.112 = C

19.113

Guidance Notes accompanying regulations are:

- [ ] A: the health and safety rules as laid down by the employer
- [ ] B: a CITB-approved guide book on health and safety
- [ ] C: a set of health and safety guidelines provided by suppliers
- [ ] D: advice on complying with legislation issued by the Health and Safety Executive

19.114

According to Health and Safety Executive figures, most accidents involving site transport are caused by vehicles:

- [ ] A: speeding
- [ ] B: ignoring one-way systems
- [ ] C: reversing
- [ ] D: being used by unqualified drivers

19.115

The significant findings of risk assessments must be recorded when more than a certain number of people are employed. How many?

- [ ] A: 3 or more
- [ ] B: 5 or more
- [ ] C: 6 or more
- [ ] D: 7 or more

19.116

Which two of the following factors must you consider when providing first-aid facilities on site?

- [ ] A: The cost of first-aid equipment
- [ ] B: The hazards and risks that are likely to occur
- [ ] C: The nature of the work carried out
- [ ] D: The difficulty in finding time to purchase the necessary equipment
- [ ] E: The space in the site office to store the necessary equipment

19.117

Which is not classified as a major injury under Reporting of Injuries, Diseases and Dangerous Occurances Regulations?

- [ ] A: Fractured finger
- [ ] B: Temporary loss of eyesight
- [ ] C: Fractured arm
- [ ] D: Broken wrist

Answers: 19.113 = D, 19.114 = C, 19.115 = B, 19.116 = B,C, 19.117 = A

19.118

What must a sub-contractor provide you with in relation to one of his employees who is 17 years old?

- [ ] A: The employee's birth certificate
- [ ] B: HSE permission for the 17 year old to be on site
- [ ] C: Parental permission for the 17 year old to be on site
- [ ] D: A risk assessment addressing the issue of young persons

19.119

What does the term 'lower exposure action value' mean when referring to noise?

- [ ] A: Noise level at the start of the job
- [ ] B: Noise level at which the employee can request hearing protection
- [ ] C: Noise level when machines on the job first start up
- [ ] D: Noise level at which the employee must wear hearing protection

19.120

At what decibel (dBA) level does it become mandatory for an employer to establish hearing protection zones?

- [ ] A: 80 dBA
- [ ] B: 85 dBA
- [ ] C: 90 dBA
- [ ] D: 95 dBA

19.121

At what minimum noise level must you provide hearing protection to employees if they ask for it?

- [ ] A: 80 decibels
- [ ] B: 85 decibels
- [ ] C: 87 decibels
- [ ] D: 90 decibels

Answers: 19.118 = D, 19.119 = B, 19.120 = B, 19.121 = A

19.122

The significance of a weekly or daily personal noise exposure of 87 dBA is that:

- [ ] A: it is the lower action value and no action is necessary
- [ ] B: it is the upper action value and hearing protection must be issued
- [ ] C: it is the peak sound pressure and all work must stop
- [ ] D: it is the exposure limit value and must not be exceeded

19.123

The Health and Safety Information for Employees Regulations require that employees be informed about specific matters of health, safety and welfare in the workplace. Under the regulations, in which two ways are employers allowed to communicate this information to their employees?

- [ ] A: By displaying the approved poster
- [ ] B: Verbally during site induction
- [ ] C: By displaying a locally produced poster
- [ ] D: By issuing an approved leaflet
- [ ] E: During a toolbox talk

19.124

Which of the following items must be entered on the approved Health and Safety Law poster by, or on behalf of, the employer?

- [ ] A: Details of all emergency escape routes
- [ ] B: The identity of the first-aiders
- [ ] C: The location of all fire extinguishers
- [ ] D: The address of the local Health and Safety Executive office

19.125

If an employee is injured in an accident that results in time off work, when must it be reported to the Health and Safety Executive under the Reporting of Injuries, Diseases and Dangerous Occurrences Regulations?

- [ ] A: When over half a day is lost
- [ ] B: When over 1 day is lost
- [ ] C: When over 2 days are lost
- [ ] D: When over 3 days are lost

Answers: 19.122 = D, 19.123 = A,D, 19.124 = D, 19.125 = D

19.126

What is regarded as the last resort for someone's safety when working at height?

- [ ] A: Safety harness
- [ ] B: Mobile elevating work platform
- [ ] C: Mobile tower scaffold
- [ ] D: Access tower scaffold

19.127

Before planning for anyone to enter a confined space, what should be the first consideration of the responsible person?

- [ ] A: Has the atmosphere in the confined space been tested?
- [ ] B: Has a safe means of access and egress been established?
- [ ] C: Is there an alternative method of doing the work?
- [ ] D: Have all who intend to enter the confined space been properly trained?

19.128

Every demolition contractor undertaking demolition operations must first appoint:

- [ ] A: a competent person to supervise the work
- [ ] B: a sub-contractor to strip out the buildings
- [ ] C: a safety officer to check on health and safety compliance
- [ ] D: a quantity surveyor to price the extras

19.129

Which two of the following documents refer to the specific hazards associated with demolition work in confined spaces?

- [ ] A: A safety policy
- [ ] B: A permit-to-work
- [ ] C: A risk assessment
- [ ] D: A scaffolding permit
- [ ] E: The HSE Health and Safety Law poster

19.130

With regard to the safe method of working, what is the most important subject of induction training for demolition operatives?

- [ ] A: Working hours on the site
- [ ] B: Explanation of the method statement
- [ ] C: Location of welfare facilities
- [ ] D: COSHH assessments

Answers: 19.126 = A, 19.127 = C, 19.128 = A, 19.129 = B,C, 19.130 = B

19.131

When asbestos material is suspected in buildings to be demolished, what is the first priority?

- [ ] A: A competent person carries out an asbestos survey
- [ ] B: Notify the HSE of the possible presence of asbestos
- [ ] C: Remove and dispose of the asbestos
- [ ] D: Employ a licensed asbestos remover

19.132

Which of the following items of PPE provides the lowest level of protection when working in dusty conditions?

- [ ] A: Half-mask dust respirator
- [ ] B: Positive pressure powered respirator
- [ ] C: Compressed airline breathing apparatus
- [ ] D: Self-contained breathing apparatus

19.133

Which two of the following would be suitable to use when cutting coated steelwork?

- [ ] A: A disposable dust-mask
- [ ] B: Positive pressure powered respirator
- [ ] C: High-efficiency dust respirator
- [ ] D: Ventilated helmet respirator
- [ ] E: Respiratory protection is not required

19.134

Which asbestos material is classified as 'non-notifiable' for removal works?

- [ ] A: Asbestos cement
- [ ] B: Asbestos insulation/coatings
- [ ] C: Asbestos insulation board
- [ ] D: Asbestos pipe lagging

19.135

How often should lifting equipment that is not used to lift people be thoroughly examined?

- [ ] A: Once every 6 months
- [ ] B: At least twice a year
- [ ] C: A minimum of once a year
- [ ] D: Every 10 years

Answers: 19.131 = A, 19.132 = A, 19.133 = B,D, 19.134 = A, 19.135 = C

20 Professionally Qualified Person – Design

20.1

Which piece of health and safety legislation always places duties on a construction designer?

- [ ] A: The Construction (Design and Management) Regulations
- [ ] B: The Health and Safety (Display Screen Equipment) Regulations
- [ ] C: The Personal Protective Equipment Regulations
- [ ] D: The Construction (Head Protection) Regulations

20.2

In addition to the Construction (Design and Management) Regulations, designers need to comply with which piece of health and safety legislation that affects those implementing or using the design?

- [ ] A: The Health and Safety (Display Screen Equipment) Regulations
- [ ] B: The Workplace (Health, Safety and Welfare) Regulations
- [ ] C: The Personal Protective Equipment Regulations
- [ ] D: The Health and Safety (First Aid) Regulations

20.3

In addition to the Construction (Design and Management) Regulations, which other health and safety regulations should influence the design activity?

- [ ] A: The Control of Vibration at Work Regulations
- [ ] B: The Construction Workplace Design Regulations
- [ ] C: The Workplace (Health, Safety and Welfare) Regulations
- [ ] D: The Construction First Aid at Work Regulations

20.4

Under which of these circumstances would you not have legal responsibility for the safety of the design under the Construction (Design and Management) Regulations?

- [ ] A: A design you prepare directly yourself as a sole practitioner
- [ ] B: Further development of an outline scheme designed by a client
- [ ] C: A design produced by another consultant employed by the client
- [ ] D: A design prepared by a former practice that the client now wants you to re-work

Answers: 20.1 = A, 20.2 = B, 20.3 = C, 20.4 = C

20.5

Which health and safety legislation, other than the Construction (Design and Management) Regulations, applies to the risk management of construction work?

- [ ] A: The Health and Safety (Display Screen Equipment) Regulations
- [ ] B: The Workplace Health, Safety and Welfare Regulations
- [ ] C: The Management of Health and Safety at Work Regulations
- [ ] D: The Building Regulations

20.6

Under the Construction (Design and Management) Regulations the duty to apply the principles of prevention rests with which duty holders?

- [ ] A: Designers and clients
- [ ] B: Contractors and Principal contractors
- [ ] C: The CDM Co-ordinator
- [ ] D: Designers and all other duty holders

20.7

With regard to occupational health, the requirements of which of the following legislation need not be considered during design work for construction work?

- [ ] A: The Control of Substances Hazardous to Health Regulations
- [ ] B: The Control of Asbestos Regulations
- [ ] C: The Construction Products Regulations
- [ ] D: The Manual Handling Operations Regulations

20.8

Which legislation, other than the Construction (Design and Management) Regulations, will always apply to design work?

- [ ] A: The Health and Safety (Display Screen Equipment) Regulations
- [ ] B: The Health and Safety at Work Act
- [ ] C: The Construction (Head Protection) Regulations
- [ ] D: The Confined Spaces Regulations

Answers: 20.5 = C, 20.6 = D, 20.7 = C, 20.8 = B

20.9

Regulation 11(1) of the Construction (Design and Management) Regulations requires designers to only commence work if:

- [ ] A: Clients are supplied with information about the client's duties under the CDM Regulations
- [ ] B: Their contracts with clients address the client's obligations under the CDM Regulations
- [ ] C: The Health and Safety Executive is notified of the project before a design is prepared
- [ ] D: Clients are aware of the client's duties under the CDM Regulations before design work is started

20.10

Under the Construction (Design and Management) regulations on a notifiable project, what should a designer do if a CDM Co-ordinator is not appointed?

- [ ] A: Work on the initial design only
- [ ] B: Work to the client's brief
- [ ] C: Work on all project design
- [ ] D: All of the other answers

20.11

When does a designer need to take steps to ensure that the client is aware of their duties under the Construction (Design and Management) Regulations?

- [ ] A: Before issuing the first invoice
- [ ] B: Before commencing design work
- [ ] C: Before starting on site
- [ ] D: Before submitting a planning application

20.12

Under the Construction (Design and Management) Regulations, where a project is not notifiable, what must a designer do before preparing a design?

- [ ] A: Ensure that a fee agreement is in place
- [ ] B: Ensure that a CDM co-ordinator is appointed
- [ ] C: Ensure that clients are aware of their duties
- [ ] D: Ensure that a principal contractor is appointed

Answers: 20.9 = D, 20.10 = A, 20.11 = B, 20.12 = C

20.13

A client is seeking a fee proposal from you, supported by sketches. What steps do you take under the Construction (Design and Management) Regulations before you submit your proposal?

- [ ] A: To calculate your reasonable fee
- [ ] B: To estimate the resources required for the project
- [ ] C: To notify the Health and Safety Executive about the project
- [ ] D: To ensure that clients are aware of their duties

20.14

Under the Construction (Design and Management) Regulations, a designer has specifically to consider the health and safety of which categories of person that might be affected by their work when preparing a design?

- [ ] A: Other designers, construction and maintenance workers, the public and site visitors
- [ ] B: Workers engaged in construction, cleaning and maintenance plus site visitors and members of the public
- [ ] C: Workers engaged in construction cleaning and maintenance plus the public and those using the structure as a workplace
- [ ] D: Construction workers, designers, site visitors members of the public and those using the structure as a place of work

20.15

As a summary of the designer's duties to manage risk under the Construction (Design and Management) Regulations, ERIC stands for:

- [ ] A: employ, reduce, inform, control
- [ ] B: ensure, reduce, inform, control
- [ ] C: eliminate, reduce, inform, control
- [ ] D: educate, reduce, inform, control

20.16

As a summary of the designer's duties to manage risk under the Construction (Design and Management) Regulations, ERIC stands for:

- [ ] A: eliminate, inform, control
- [ ] B: eliminate, remodel, inform, control
- [ ] C: eliminate, recalculate, inform, control
- [ ] D: eliminate, reduce, inform, control

Answers: 20.13 = D, 20.14 = C, 20.15 = C, 20.16 = D

20.17

As a summary of the designer's duties to manage risk under the Construction (Design and Management) Regulations, ERIC stands for:

- A: eliminate, reduce, inform, control
- B: eliminate, reduce, infer, control
- C: eliminate, reduce, imply, control
- D: eliminate, reduce, induct, control

20.18

As a summary of the designer's duties to manage risk under the Construction (Design and Management) Regulations, ERIC stands for:

- A: eliminate, reduce, inform, comply
- B: eliminate, reduce, inform, control
- C: eliminate, reduce, inform, cost
- D: eliminate, reduce, inform, co-ordinate

20.19

Which of the following will not eliminate significant construction hazards?

- A: Locating former roof-level plant at ground level
- B: Moving the building envelope so that piling misses contaminated made-up ground
- C: Designing pull-off areas for motorway plant maintenance vehicles
- D: Operatives working at an unprotected, high-level leading edge wearing a safety harness and fall-arrest lanyard

20.20

As a designer, what is the most effective action you can take to prevent workers falling from height while carrying out construction and maintenance work?

- A: Leave the decision on construction methods to the principal contractor
- B: Ensure details of risky operations are included in the health and safety plan
- C: Educate the workforce to be more careful while working at height
- D: Produce design solutions that eliminate the need for working at height

Answers: 20.17 = A, 20.18 = B, 20.19 = D, 20.20 = D

20.21

Which statement is not a requirement for designers under the Construction (Design and Management) Regulations?

- [ ] A: Designers should provide information for the health and safety file
- [ ] B: Designers must co-operate with the CDM Co-ordinator
- [ ] C: Designers must take account of The Workplace (Health, Safety and Welfare) Regulations
- [ ] D: Designers must manage the safety of their designs on site

20.22

Which of the following does not eliminate significant construction hazards?

- [ ] A: Specifying working at height from an elevating platform
- [ ] B: Re-routing a service run to avoid an asbestos panel
- [ ] C: Designing pre-cast holding down bolts
- [ ] D: Waiting for a shared occupancy building to become empty before construction work starts

20.23

Under the Construction (Design and Management) Regulations, a designer must give adequate regard to which of these design considerations?

- [ ] A: Avoiding foreseeable claims for health and safety equipment by contractors
- [ ] B: Avoiding variation orders on health and safety issues
- [ ] C: Avoiding foreseeable risks to the health and safety of persons
- [ ] D: Avoiding foreseeable risks to the project programme

20.24

Under the Construction (Design and Management) Regulations, to what standard of compliance must designers work to eliminate foreseeable construction risks arising from their designs?

- [ ] A: Construction risks must be eliminated at all costs
- [ ] B: Construction risks must be eliminated so far as is practicable
- [ ] C: Construction risks need not be eliminated
- [ ] D: Construction risks must be eliminated so far as is reasonably practicable

Answers: 20.21 = D, 20.22 = A, 20.23 = C, 20.24 = D

20.25

When considering the contribution that a designer can make to construction workers' wellbeing, they should try to:

- [ ] A: eliminate the foreseeable safety and health hazards
- [ ] B: get the building watertight as soon as possible
- [ ] C: give priority to prefabrication
- [ ] D: specify appropriate personal protective equipment

20.26

What is the highest priority under the principles of prevention and protection?

- [ ] A: To use new technology
- [ ] B: To avoid foreseeable risks on site
- [ ] C: To specify collective protective measures
- [ ] D: To ensure that workers know the risks they will face on site

20.27

Why is the elimination of a design-related construction hazard the most effective design risk management solution?

- [ ] A: Because the potential for harm has been removed
- [ ] B: Because it will save the client money
- [ ] C: Because the CDM Co-ordinator will be satisfied
- [ ] D: Because it meets the conditions of your professional indemnity insurance policy

20.28

Why is the elimination of a design-related construction hazard the most effective design risk management solution?

- [ ] A: There is less to notify to the Health and Safety Executive during the design phase
- [ ] B: Significant potential for harm has been removed from the construction process
- [ ] C: I will not be asked about it by the CDM Co-ordinator again
- [ ] D: It meets our office quality assurance policy

Answers: 20.25 = A, 20.26 = B, 20.27 = A, 20.28 = B

20.29

Which of the following can designers significantly influence though the design process?

- [ ] A: Elimination or reduction of health hazards faced by construction workers
- [ ] B: Improvements in the safe behaviour of construction workers
- [ ] C: Management of the Principal Contractor's site safety system
- [ ] D: Improvements in construction workers' knowledge of safe systems of work

20.30

Which of the following is the least important justification for recording outcomes of any hazard elimination throughout the design process?

- [ ] A: So that the client's safety advisor can check and see that design team's fee levels and resources are adequate
- [ ] B: So that other designers in the project can appreciate the risk management decisions made before
- [ ] C: To demonstrate effective risk co-ordinations and co-operation
- [ ] D: To have an audit trail if the Health and Safety Executive ask us questions

20.31

Which of the following is an appropriate way of recording hazards that designers have eliminated during the design development?

- [ ] A: In the health and safety file
- [ ] B: In a manual prepared for the structure
- [ ] C: In a semi-quantitative risk assessment
- [ ] D: In a project or risk register

20.32

Where designers are not able to combat risks to health and safety at source, they should as the next priority:

- [ ] A: tell construction workers about the risk and how they should reasonably protect themselves
- [ ] B: avoid any further design input and specify the appropriate personal protective equipment
- [ ] C: avoid foreseeable risks and give priority to measures that will protect all persons at work
- [ ] D: avoid dealing with the risk and let the principal contractor manage it

Answers: 20.29 = A, 20.30 = A, 20.31 = D, 20.32 = C

20.33

The reduction of foreseeable risk:

- [ ] A: has a higher priority than the elimination of hazards
- [ ] B: is not a concern for designers
- [ ] C: is a matter for the principal contractor alone
- [ ] D: has a lower priority than the elimination of hazards

20.34

Under the general principles of prevention, what is generally accepted as the least effective option that a designer can take to protect construction workers?

- [ ] A: Specify construction processes which protect groups of workers rather than individuals
- [ ] B: Provide information to the contractor on residual risks to enable them to give instructions to their workers
- [ ] C: Amend your design to replace dangerous construction processes with less dangerous ones
- [ ] D: Amend your design to eliminate hazards from construction processes

20.35

Under the general principles of prevention, what is generally accepted as the most effective option that a designer can take to protect construction workers?

- [ ] A: Specify construction processes which protect groups of workers rather than individuals
- [ ] B: Provide information to the contractor on residual risks to enable them to give instructions to their workers
- [ ] C: Amend your design to replace dangerous construction processes with less dangerous ones
- [ ] D: Amend your design to eliminate hazards from construction processes

20.36

Assuming all other factors are equal, which of the following solutions provides the greatest reduction in exposure to risk?

- [ ] A: A two-person operation to clean a structure once every 2 years
- [ ] B: A two-person operation to clean a structure once a year
- [ ] C: A four-person operation to clean a structure every 6 months
- [ ] D: A one-person operation to clean a structure every month

Answers: 20.33 = D, 20.34 = B, 20.35 = D, 20.36 = A

20.37

When considering plans for a project site layout, which of the following provides the best design solution for reducing risks related to transport and access?

- [ ] A: The project manager decides once all other design details are complete
- [ ] B: Show a one-way traffic system on drawings and provide for separated pedestrian routes
- [ ] C: Provide general arrangement drawings so that the contractor could consider the site traffic system at tender stage
- [ ] D: Avoid the need for some vehicle movements on site by requiring more materials to be off-loaded manually outside the site

20.38

You are designing a grouting system. Which of the following would be the best way to find out more about the health risks involved in the design, and how to avoid them?

- [ ] A: Talking through the supplier's material safety data sheets with a specialist contractor
- [ ] B: The specialist trade contractor will choose the solution once its performance has been specified
- [ ] C: Talking to the sales representative at your usual trade wholesaler
- [ ] D: Leaving it for the Health and Safety Executive to give advice about it when they come to site

20.39

Which of these techniques is least effective in reducing health or safety risks on site?

- [ ] A: Off site prefabrication of building components
- [ ] B: Significantly reducing the need for deep excavations
- [ ] C: Reducing the need for work at height
- [ ] D: Specifying the PPE to be provided to construction workers

Answers: 20.37 = B, 20.38 = A, 20.39 = D

20.40

Which one of the following is not a relevant option for reducing the risk to construction workers?

- [ ] A: Reduce the number of workers
- [ ] B: Reduce the duration of the work
- [ ] C: Reduce the cost of work equipment
- [ ] D: Reduce the frequency of a maintenance activity

20.41

Which phrase in Regulation 11 of the Construction (Design and Management) Regulations defines the extent to which designers have to reduce the risks of their designs?

- [ ] A: Responsibly practicable
- [ ] B: Reasonably practicable
- [ ] C: Unreasonably practicable
- [ ] D: Foreseeably practicable

20.42

Where significant or unusual residual construction process risks remain, having applied the general principles of prevention, a designer is required to:

- [ ] A: tell the contractor how to manage the works
- [ ] B: specify personal protective equipment
- [ ] C: take reasonable steps to provide sufficient information about them
- [ ] D: develop method statements for the contractor to instruct their workers

20.43

Under the Construction (Design and Management) Regulations, design information about residual risks of a completed structure needs to be put in the:

- [ ] A: construction phase health and safety plan
- [ ] B: O&M manuals
- [ ] C: manuals prepared for completed structures
- [ ] D: health and safety file

Answers: 20.40 = C, 20.41 = B, 20.42 = C, 20.43 = D

20.44

Having applied the general principles of prevention, designers must take all reasonable steps to provide sufficient information about the design aspects to assist:

- [ ] A: the client, other designers and contractors to take them into account
- [ ] B: designers and contractors to meet their contractual obligations
- [ ] C: the CDM co-ordinator to take over the responsibility for design
- [ ] D: the principal contractor to take over the responsibility for design

20.45

The provision by designers of health and safety information under the Construction (Design and Management) Regulations allows:

- [ ] A: the designer to work on another project
- [ ] B: contractors to allocate adequate site resources to manage the risks
- [ ] C: the designer to meet their obligations under the project contract
- [ ] D: the designer to keep the CDM co-ordinator reasonably happy

20.46

Who is responsible for preparing the Health and Safety file?

- [ ] A: The CDM Co-ordinator
- [ ] B: Whoever the client has commissioned to prepare it
- [ ] C: The lead designer
- [ ] D: The principal contractor

20.47

Under the Construction (Design and Management) Regulations, which list describes all the duty holders who must provide health and safety information?

- [ ] A: The client, designers, the CDM Co-ordinator and all contractors
- [ ] B: The CDM Co-ordinator, designers and client's agent
- [ ] C: Designers, contractors and the planning authority
- [ ] D: The CDM Co-ordinator, contractors and principal contractor

Answers: 20.44 = A, 20.45 = B, 20.46 = A, 20.47 = A

20.48

What is likely to be the least effective way of informing the principal contractor about residual health risks in your design?

- [ ] A: Adding notes to the specification
- [ ] B: Supplying material safety data sheets
- [ ] C: Adding notes to drawings
- [ ] D: A brief telephone conversation

20.49

What is the critical reason for supplying health or safety information?

- [ ] A: To comply with procedures
- [ ] B: It is a requirement of the role of the CDM co-ordinator
- [ ] C: To communicate on risk issues
- [ ] D: To satisfy the Health and Safety Executive

20.50

For a notifiable project, what health and safety information must be supplied with a completed design for an alteration to an existing structure?

- [ ] A: An existing health and safety file and the health and safety folder
- [ ] B: An existing health and safety file and pre-construction information
- [ ] C: The health and safety plan and the health and safety folder
- [ ] D: The health and safety planner and the building manual

20.51

Under the Construction (Design and Management) Regulations, designers are required to:

- [ ] A: co-ordinate the work of the CDM co-ordinator and other designers
- [ ] B: manage the work of the CDM co-ordinator and other designers
- [ ] C: co-operate with the CDM co-ordinator and other designers
- [ ] D: manage contractors and others in terms of health and safety

Answers: 20.48 = D, 20.49 = C, 20.50 = B, 20.51 = C

20.52

Under the Construction (Design and Management) Regulations, designers are required to co-operate with each other so that:

- [ ] A: the CDM co-ordinator is happy and can report back to the client
- [ ] B: each designer can fulfil their duties under the regulations
- [ ] C: the client will pay their fees, especially if safety issues are raised
- [ ] D: all of the other answers

20.53

Under the Construction (Design and Management) Regulations, designers are required to co-operate with the CDM co-ordinator so that:

- [ ] A: the CDM Co-ordinator can comply with the requirements of the regulations
- [ ] B: the client can pay the CDM co-ordinator's fees in accordance with appointment requirements
- [ ] C: the QA auditors can issue a compliance certificate to the CDM co-ordinator
- [ ] D: the CDM Co-ordinator can take the credit for the designer's work

20.54

Under the Construction (Design and Management) Regulations a designer's primary duty is to:

- [ ] A: make any design changes the CDM co-ordinator asks for
- [ ] B: alter their designs that will allow other designers to meet their obligations under the regulations
- [ ] C: issue their fee invoices in response to design risk reductions
- [ ] D: modify their designs to allow the contractor to build the project more safely

20.55

Designers must co-operate with the CDM co-ordinator because it is something:

- [ ] A: for the design team to decide
- [ ] B: that regulations do not require
- [ ] C: the regulations require
- [ ] D: something the regulations imply but do not state

Answers: 20.52 = B, 20.53 = A, 20.54 = D, 20.55 = C

20.56

Which of the following are two ways suggested by the Approved Code of Practice for encouraging designers to co-operate with other duty holders?

- [ ] A: Encourage the client to make early appointments of design teams
- [ ] B: Ensure that designers take account of unforseeable hazards and risks
- [ ] C: Setting up an integrated team involving designers, principal contractor and other relevant contractors
- [ ] D: Ensure that the design teams have allocated sufficient time and resources
- [ ] E: Agree a common approach to risk reduction during design development

20.57

The design team is aware that the client has data on the presence of asbestos for an existing structure. On the insistence of the client the design team omits reference to this in a work package provided to a contractor appointed to work on the structure. In this circumstance the design team and the client have acted:

- [ ] A: reasonably practicably
- [ ] B: illegally
- [ ] C: legally
- [ ] D: with adequate regard

20.58

Under the Construction (Design and Management) Regulations, who has a responsibility to ensure that competent duty holders are appointed?

- [ ] A: The CDM Co-ordinator
- [ ] B: The client
- [ ] C: Anyone appointing a designer or contractor
- [ ] D: The principal contractor

20.59

If a designer appoints another designer or a contractor, the Construction (Design and Management) Regulations require them to:

- [ ] A: agree production and payment terms
- [ ] B: ensure the competence of the designer or contractor they appoint
- [ ] C: be sure that they carry out their duties under the regulations
- [ ] D: be satisfied that they are competent

Answers: 20.56 = C,E, 20.57 = B, 20.58 = B, 20.59 = D

20.60

By when should a designer have taken reasonable steps to establish the competence of another designer they are appointing?

- [ ] A: Before arranging for a design to be prepared
- [ ] B: Before arranging for a planning application
- [ ] C: Before arranging to go out to tender
- [ ] D: Before arranging for the client to appoint them

20.61

Under the Construction (Design and Management) Regulations, who has the responsibility for ensuring that project arrangements are in place for the allocation of sufficient resources?

- [ ] A: The CDM co-ordinator
- [ ] B: The client
- [ ] C: The lead designer
- [ ] D: The principal contractor

20.62

Under the Construction (Design and Management) Regulations, the CDM co-ordinator:

- [ ] A: must give suitable and sufficient advice and assistance to the client
- [ ] B: must approve the appointment of designers
- [ ] C: must provide advice about designers' competence and resources if the client asks
- [ ] D: is not required to check competence and resources

20.63

On a notifiable project, which duty holder must take all reasonable steps to identify and collect pre-construction information?

- [ ] A: The client
- [ ] B: The lead designer
- [ ] C: The CDM co-ordinator
- [ ] D: The principal contractor

Answers: 20.60 = A, 20.61 = B, 20.62 = A, 20.63 = C

20.64

In what circumstances must a construction phase health and safety plan be prepared?

- [ ] A: Whenever the Construction (Design and Management) Regulations apply
- [ ] B: Only if the client asks them to do so
- [ ] C: Only if the lead designer asks them to do so
- [ ] D: Whenever the project is notifiable

20.65

Who is responsible for the management of health and safety on site?

- [ ] A: The client
- [ ] B: The designers
- [ ] C: The principal contractor
- [ ] D: The CDM Co-ordinator

20.66

Under the Construction (Design and Management) Regulations, which of the following is not defined as design work?

- [ ] A: Demolition and dismantling work prior to an archaeological project
- [ ] B: Specifying decorative finishes
- [ ] C: Site preparation prior to the excavation of an open-cast coal mine
- [ ] D: Detailing a reinforced concrete structure

20.67

Which one of the following is not considered to be a designer under the Construction (Design and Management) Regulations?

- [ ] A: A client demanding a specific detail
- [ ] B: A specialist subcontractor
- [ ] C: Someone preparing a bill of quantities
- [ ] D: A quantity surveyor measuring contract progress

20.68

Under the Construction (Design and Management) Regulations, when do designers need to manage risk?

- [ ] A: For any design that they undertake
- [ ] B: Only if there are no significant risks in their design
- [ ] C: When they put the tender package together
- [ ] D: Only if the CDM co-ordinator asks them to do so

Answers: 20.64 = D, 20.65 = C, 20.66 = C, 20.67 = D, 20.68 = A

20.69

In meeting the risk management objectives of the Construction (Design and Management) Regulations, which statement summarises the best project attitude for improving health and safety on construction sites?

- [ ] A: Only the CDM co-ordinator can eliminate hazards
- [ ] B: Only the client has the budget to eliminate hazards
- [ ] C: Designers and contractors can eliminate hazards
- [ ] D: Designers create hazards and contractors eliminate them

20.70

On notifiable projects, when do the Construction (Design and Management) Regulations require clients to appoint a CDM co-ordinator?

- [ ] A: As soon as possible after planning permission is received
- [ ] B: As soon as is practicable after initial design work has begun
- [ ] C: Just before going out to tender
- [ ] D: Before or just after construction work starts on site

20.71

When do designers need to start considering their duties under the Construction (Design and Management) Regulations?

- [ ] A: When they prepare the tender drawings
- [ ] B: When the CDM co-ordinator asks
- [ ] C: From the start of design
- [ ] D: When detailed design begins

20.72

Design for domestic clients:

- [ ] A: is not included as a designer's duty under the Construction (Design and Management) Regulations
- [ ] B: is only included as a designer's duty under the Construction (Design and Management) Regulations if demolition is involved
- [ ] C: is included as a designer's duty under the Construction (Design and Management) Regulations if the site work lasts 30 days
- [ ] D: is included as a designer's duty under the Construction (Design and Management) Regulations

Answers: 20.69 = C, 20.70 = B, 20.71 = C, 20.72 = D

20.73

Initially, who is most likely to hold most information about the health and safety constraints of the site?

- [ ] A: The CDM Co-ordinator
- [ ] B: The principal contractor
- [ ] C: The Health and Safety Executive
- [ ] D: The client

20.74

Under the Construction (Design and Management) Regulations, during which of these project phases do you have a legal duty for the safety of your design?

- [ ] A: Feasibility
- [ ] B: Detailed design
- [ ] C: Construction phase
- [ ] D: All of the other answers

20.75

According to the CDM Regulations' Approved Code of Practice, which one of these issues does not need to be considered by designers?

- [ ] A: Design issues that are not obvious to a competent contractor or other designers
- [ ] B: The client's awareness of their duties
- [ ] C: Possible future uses of the structure that cannot be foreseen
- [ ] D: Issues likely to be difficult to manage

20.76

Which of the following duty holders only have to be appointed by the client if a project is notifiable under the Construction (Design and Management) Regulations?

- [ ] A: A designer and a CDM co-ordinator
- [ ] B: A CDM co-ordinator and a client's agent
- [ ] C: A principal contractor and a CDM co-ordinator
- [ ] D: A client's agent and a designer

20.77

The most significant influences on eliminating hazards and reducing risks can generally be made by the:

- [ ] A: principal contractor during the construction period
- [ ] B: planning authority before going out to tender
- [ ] C: designer in the early stages of design
- [ ] D: CDM co-ordinator at any time during the contract

Answers: 20.73 = D, 20.74 = D, 20.75 = C, 20.76 = C, 20.77 = C

20.78

It is often stated that many accidents occur because of decisions taken before construction actually starts. This problem could be overcome if:

- [ ] A: the principal contractor did a better job of managing health and safety on site
- [ ] B: CDM co-ordinators are more proactive in the investigation of accidents that occur
- [ ] C: the client exerted more control over contractors to tackle where the risks actually arise
- [ ] D: designers respond to the contribution they can make in reducing causes of accidents

20.79

How can construction workers be harmed by the actions of others who are not on site?

- [ ] A: By foreseeable risks not being avoided by designers where practical to do so
- [ ] B: By workers fooling around
- [ ] C: By principal contractors not carrying out safety inspections
- [ ] D: By clients not paying a big enough contract sum to the principal contractor

20.80

Who is responsible for managing health and safety on site?

- [ ] A: The CDM co-ordinator
- [ ] B: The principal contractor
- [ ] C: The client
- [ ] D: The designer

20.81

You read the sensational headline 'Designers cause deaths on site'. Which statement more accurately and clearly states the causes of site accidents?

- [ ] A: Site accidents have many causes but designers, contractors, clients and workers can all reduce risks
- [ ] B: Site accidents have many causes but designers are so removed from site that they cannot affect risks in the workplace
- [ ] C: Site accidents have many causes but only the principal contractor can remove or manage risks
- [ ] D: Site accidents have many causes but the client has complete responsibility for risks

Answers: 20.78 = D, 20.79 = A, 20.80 = B, 20.81 = A

20.82

With regard to procurement routes, the Construction (Design and Management) Regulations and the Approved Code of Practice:

- [ ] A: do not apply to new forms of contract created since 1995
- [ ] B: do not apply to PFI projects
- [ ] C: do not deal with design and build
- [ ] D: apply to all construction work

20.83

From the date of CDM 2007 coming into force, what is the maximum permitted period of time that duty holders could still have to work with a CDM 1994 Client's Agent?

- [ ] A: 1 year
- [ ] B: 3 years
- [ ] C: 5 years
- [ ] D: 7 years

20.84

What is the main cause of death on construction sites?

- [ ] A: Electrocution
- [ ] B: Drowning
- [ ] C: Falls from height
- [ ] D: Weil's disease (Leptospirosis)

20.85

Which of the following health risks has resulted in the death of the most construction workers?

- [ ] A: Hand-arm vibration
- [ ] B: Hardwood dust
- [ ] C: Weil's disease (Leptospirosis)
- [ ] D: Asbestos

20.86

Statistically, which of the following is the most significant construction risk that a designer can reasonably influence?

- [ ] A: Being struck by moving vehicles
- [ ] B: Noise
- [ ] C: Drowning
- [ ] D: Electricity

Answers: 20.82 = D, 20.83 = C, 20.84 = C, 20.85 = D, 20.86 = A

20.87

A correct statement on significant construction risks would be that they:

- [ ] A: need to be controlled by the CDM Co-ordinator
- [ ] B: need to be considered by designers when undertaking their designs
- [ ] C: are the **direct** responsibility of the client
- [ ] D: are a cause for concern beyond the control of the project team

20.88

Of the following, the most authoritative source of information on designers' duties under the Construction (Design and Management) Regulations is:

- [ ] A: British Standards
- [ ] B: approved documents to the Building Regulations
- [ ] C: The Approved Code of Practice
- [ ] D: institution journals

20.89

Of the following, the most authoritative source of information on designers' duties under the Construction (Design and Management) Regulations is:

- [ ] A: British Standards
- [ ] B: approved documents to the Building Regulations
- [ ] C: institution journals
- [ ] D: the Health and Safety Executive website

20.90

In which of the following can you find specific examples and information about designers' duties under the Construction (Design and Management) Regulations?

- [ ] A: CIRIA Report C604 work sector guidance for designers
- [ ] B: British Standards
- [ ] C: Approved documents to the Building Regulations
- [ ] D: Institution journals

Answers: 20.87 = B, 20.88 = C, 20.89 = D, 20.90 = A

20.91

Which of the following is a good reason for designers obtaining and communicating information on construction health risks?

- [ ] A: Many construction workers do not know enough about construction health risks
- [ ] B: Construction workers do not always understand the long-term effects on their health of particular construction processes
- [ ] C: Ill health in construction workers is more common than traumatic injuries
- [ ] D: All of the other answers

20.92

Which sector of the construction industry has the highest fatal accident incident rate?

- [ ] A: Civil engineering sites
- [ ] B: Demolition sites
- [ ] C: Green field sites
- [ ] D: Refurbishment sites

20.93

In what circumstances do contractors have duties under the Construction (Design and Management) Regulations?

- [ ] A: Only if their work will last more than 30 days
- [ ] B: On all construction projects
- [ ] C: On all work for domestic clients only
- [ ] D: Only where demolition is involved

Answers: 20.91 = D, 20.92 = D, 20.93 = B

Acknowledgements

ConstructionSkills wishes to acknowledge the assistance offered by the following organisations in the development of health and safety testing:

Health and Safety Test Question Sub-Committee

ConstructionSkills (NI)

Construction Employers Federation Limited (CEF NI)

Driving Standards Agency

Heating and Ventilating Contractors' Association (HVCA)

Highways Agency

Joint Industry Board – Plumbing, Mechanical and Electrical Services

Lift and Escalator Industry Association (LEIA)

Management Board of the Construction Skills Certification Scheme

National Demolition Training Group

Scottish and Northern Ireland Joint Industry Board for the Plumbing Industry

Notes

Notes

Notes

Notes

Notes

Notes

Notes

Notes

Notes

University of
South Wales
Prifysgol
De Cymru
Library Service

Notes

Notes